Orange

COUNTY

CHRONICLES

Orange

COUNTY
CHRONICLES

Stories from a
Historic Virginia County

PATRICIA LaLand

THE
History
PRESS

Published by The History Press

Charleston, SC 29403

www.historypress.net

Cover image: The fields at the Briary in Rapidan.

All images courtesy of the author unless otherwise noted.

First published 2011

ISBN 9781540234964

LaLand, Patricia.

Orange County chronicles : stories from a historic Virginia county / Patricia LaLand.

p. cm.

ISBN 9781540234964

1. Orange County (Va.)--History--Anecdotes. I. Title.

F232.O6L35 2011

975.5'372--dc23

2011044641

This book is dedicated to my family, whom I deeply love, with special thanks to good friends who were instrumental in making it happen. They are newswoman and editor Gwen Woolf from the Fredericksburg Free Lance-Star *newspaper and local Virginia gentlemen Alan Shotwell and Duff Green; a particular thank-you goes to Will McKay of* The History Press *for his patience and good nature.*

Contents

CONTENTS

Preface

When I came to Orange in the autumn of 1989, little did I know the degree to which Orange County would catch and hold me while generously opening its personal and family stories to me. Being a columnist for a monthly publication for a few years sent me to people who were willing to share their wisdom, their experiences and their family histories, which I had the honor and pleasure of writing down.

As a native of Seattle, Washington, where no historic events of significant national or international impact have occurred before Apple and Microsoft (well, and maybe Starbucks), I was unaware of the emotional impact of experiencing, in person, the tangible aspects of our country's relatively short but powerful history. Then the army assigned my husband to Virginia, where I ultimately spent seventeen years working at Colonial Williamsburg and studying colonial history. The excitement of having a personal touch with the past has never left, and it only grew when I came to Orange to be the assistant director at Montpelier and met people whose lives and families have been inspired by it. I am so pleased to be able to share these stories again, and I hope you will love them, too.

Pete Joyner Remembers Orange County History

Pete Joyner left a local law practice in 1982 and was later appointed clerk of the Orange County Circuit Court, a position he held for seventeen years while writing the definitive and scholarly history of the county, *The First Settlers of Orange County, Virginia, 1700–1776*.

Pete said that his two favorite subjects are history and law. "Law is history," he says, "recorded in the ownership of land and titles to land. Background to Orange County history and the development of government comes from records of the land ownership."

"Orange County is important to historians," he continued. "Theoretically, it originally contained all the land to the Pacific Ocean, but realistically, from here to the Mississippi River. I never saw it, but there is a reference to a log cabin in a park in Chicago with a plaque that identifies it as the Orange County Courthouse. You could call it an early branch office. People that far away couldn't come here to deal with their legal affairs."

"Alexander Spotswood was appointed lieutenant governor of Virginia by Queen Anne in 1712. He was a strong advocate of progress and was the only royal governor to remain here after his term ended in 1722," Pete noted. "He tried to encourage westward expansion and settlement in 1714 by taking the Knights of the Golden Horseshoe, a group that included wealthy planters, political leaders and friends,

Orange County Courthouse.

to explore the Blue Ridge mountains and awarded them land grants and gave them small golden horseshoe-shaped pins. The symbol was chosen because they had to shoe their horses to prepare them for going from the sandy soil in the Tidewater area to rocky terrain in the Piedmont region."

Pete continued: "He settled a group of German iron miners here in 1720 in Germanna and created Spotsylvania and Brunswick Counties in 1720. He was not selfless and had numerous financial interests. As Spotswood grew, Virginia grew. At one point, Orange County encompassed what are now Augusta, Culpeper, Greene, Madison and Orange counties."

As Pete noted in *The First Settlers of Orange County, Virginia, 1700–1776*:

> *Exploration into the west and southwest expanded into new states and the influence of Virginia and Orange County grew as well. The wealth*

of Virginia lay in land ownership and primogeniture was the rule at that point, meaning that the eldest son inherited the bulk of the property. Early genealogical records show that the rest of the sons tended to leave on their own and, needing to find new land for themselves, resulted in further expansion of settlement.

Zachary Taylor's father, for instance, was a younger son and was given a land grant in Kentucky for service in the Revolutionary War. Zachary was born in 1874 when the family still lived in Orange County so we can claim him as a native son. However, it was the custom for a woman to go to her parents' home for the birth of her first child, thus, despite the fact that Orange County was the lifelong home of James Madison, we lost claim to his birth to Caroline County.

As settlement spread west, county courthouses brought population and business and increased the surrounding land value. Except for the small settlement at Germanna, which could hardly be called a town, there was nothing resembling development in what is now Orange County until the "Village at Orange Courthouse" began to come to life in the late 1700s.

The Orange County Courthouse had several locations but originally was located at Black Walnut Run. Henry Willis offered the land for it. He was the first clerk of court and the sessions were held in his house although he lived in Frederick County.

The Taylors became the most influential family, meaning the largest landowners here, so in 1752 the courthouse moved to Orange where it now remains. Several Taylors served as Clerks of the Court. Then the Madisons rose in importance and held that and other prominent positions.

The town of Orange, as it exists today, lies on the boundary between two major grants of land. In 1726 John Baylor of King and Queen County acquired a grant for 6,500 acres on the south side of the Rapidan at the mouth of Laurel Run. Just to the east of Baylor and also on the south side of the Rapidan, Col. James Taylor, also of King and Queen County, acquired a patent for 8,500 acres in 1722.

The Baylor tract remained relatively intact until 1804 at which time it was divided. Only the westernmost portions of the town lie within the bounds of the Baylor grant.

In 1725 Col. Taylor sold off 100 acres of his grant to James Rucker and an adjoining 100 acres to Thomas Jackson. These two parcels which together came to be known at "the Courthouse tract," became the site of the new town which grew up around the courthouse that was moved from Raccoon Ford in 1749.

In 1733 Thomas Jackson sold his 100 acre tract to William Crosthwait and in 1750 Crosthwait's son William acquired the adjoining 100 acres, thus joining the two tracts in the same family.

William Crosthwait operated a tavern, or "ordinary" on the site for which he was first granted a license by the Orange County court in 1741. When Culpeper County was split off from Orange in 1749, it was decided to move the courthouse to a more central location and the land of Timothy Crosthwait was chosen as the site. The court met for the first time in the home of Crosthwait in November, 1749 and continued to meet there until the completion of the new courthouse in 1752. Crosthwait became the new courthouse custodian as well as continuing to operate his tavern for the benefit of the "gentlemen justices" and those who made use of the court.

Gradually, around the courthouse there developed livery stables, stores and other businesses catering to the needs of those who traveled to the county seat to attend to legal business. The monthly court days came to be festivals of sorts involving the people not only in court matters but also in the conduct of all kinds of activity from horse trading and racing to cockfighting.

Politicians campaigned among the people gathered around the courthouse and dispersed drinks here and there in the hope that a vote or two might be turned in their direction. Among the early merchants at Orange Courthouse was Andrew Shepherd whose storehouse was located at the southeast corner of present East Main Street and Byrd Street and George Frazer, whose storehouse was included in the "prison bounds" established in the new county seat in 1752.

Very little development occurred until about 1800, when the Crosthwait lands surrounding the courthouse passed into the hands of Paul Verdier. In about 1806, Verdier built his home, Mount Peliso, which still stands, and began to sell off lots along Main Street, then still called the "Swift Run Road." In 1818, Verdier and his wife, Sarah, conveyed portions of his land to his sons-in-law: Richard M. Chapman, who married Maria Verdier, and Andrew Shepherd Jr., who married Susan Verdier. The Chapman land lay generally south of the Swift Run Road and east of the Gordonsville Road, now Caroline Street. The Shepherd land lay generally in the triangle formed by the Swift Run Road on the south, the Barnett's Ford Road (now Madison Road) on the west and the old road to Barnett's Ford (now May Fray Avenue) on the east.

"Spurred by the railroad which arrived in 1853, the successors of Paul Verdier continued the development of the 'Courthouse Tract' and by 1880 over 800 persons call the village home," Joyner noted. The 2010 census report showed a county population of 33,481, which includes 4,721 in the town of Orange and 1,498 in Gordonsville.

Ulysses Percy Joyner Jr. was given the nickname "Pete" by his grandmother. He grew up, fascinated by history, in Southhampton County and married the girl across the street, Martha Barham, who spent many productive years as a teacher in Orange County schools. He said, "It has been fascinating to study and be involved with history," for which Orange County can be grateful.

124 Years in Publishing

B eing born into a newspaper family is like being on a farm. You're always busy and never have an official vacation."

Duff Green's infectious grin and the sparkle in his bright blue eyes reflect the energy and responsiveness that this energetic youngest son, born in 1928 to a fourth-generation newspaper family, brings to the Orange community.

As the unofficial family historian, Duff also has at his fingertips the photo archives of the local weekly newspaper, the *Orange County Review*, for which he was the chief photographer (as well as a writer) for sixty years. The family endeavors chronicle the history of newspapering in both Culpeper and Orange Counties.

The Green family's involvement in journalism started in 1881 when James W. Green and his son, Angus McDonald Green, both attorneys, started the *Culpeper Exponent*, which became the fourth newspaper in Culpeper at the time.

Angus was elected mayor of Culpeper in 1889, but unfortunately, he died four years later at the age of thirty-three while he was working in the hayfields on his farm on a hot day in July. His younger brother, Raleigh, also a lawyer and newspaperman in Parkersburg, West Virginia, moved back to Culpeper to take his place in the law firm, and he also took on the position of editor of the *Culpeper Exponent*.

In 1912, the family purchased the *Orange Review* at auction for $500. The date of the paper's establishment is lost in the dust of time, although mention was made of it in 1887 by its competitor, the *Orange Observer*.

World War I took most of the printers into the military, and since the *Orange Review* was inconveniently located down a dusty dirt road twenty miles away from Culpeper in the town of Orange, the Greens closed it in early 1918.

Thirteen years later, it was reopened by invitation of the chamber of commerce and was run by a second newspaper-wise James W. Green, who had returned from active duty in the army, a veteran of both the Spanish-American War and World War I.

People in Orange County had the option then of reading both the *Orange County News*, being printed in Gordonsville, and the *Orange Observer*, a paper with a fifty-year publishing history.

"At that time," said Duff, "Miss Bertha Robinson owned and was running the *Orange Observer* from her home on West Main Street in Orange." Miss Bertha was a famous character in town for fifty years, known for her flowery prose that overly embellished weddings, funerals and all social activities. Several years later, both the *Orange Observer* and the *Orange County News* ceased publication.

The *Orange Review* reinvented itself in a building facing Railroad Avenue in town until it moved into the building behind it, facing Chapman Street, which had been a bakery. That building was renovated in 1905, and when paint was removed from the exterior wall, the newspaper's name, originally painted on the brick, was once again exposed.

James W. Green's newspaper and commercial printing plant business grew moderately through the Great Depression, partly because seven of his children helped run it.

In 1935, when Duff was seven years old, the family bought a small hand printing press. "They teased me and said it was for me," said Duff, "and I believed them and even learned to use it. George Smith used it in his printing business for years. I asked him if I could buy it, and he wouldn't sell it to me—which is probably a good thing because I don't know how my wife would like *that* in the living room. But when I asked George if he would leave it to me in his will, he said he would think about it."

Duff Green with the old press.

In 1941, war again took its toll on the business when three of the four sons went into active military duty, leaving thirteen-year-old Duff and his three sisters to help their father, as well as two printers who were beyond military draft age.

"We were struggling for help and working six days a week and until 6:00 p.m. on Saturday. On Sunday, our 'day off,' we came in between 1:00 p.m. and 3:00 p.m. to clean up the alley, the bathrooms and all that," said Duff. "It was a hard schedule, and I used to go to sleep in geometry class, and on Friday nights during the football games, I would sleep on the bench until I went onto the field."

"One gentleman in town purchased a subscription to the paper for every local serviceman. The *Orange County Review* was going all over the world," continued Duff. "In 1945, we were ready to go to press when W.A. Sherman, who had been listening to the radio, called to say, 'President Roosevelt died!' Thirty minutes later, we had yanked the head and put in, 'Nation Mourns.' I think we were the first newspaper to publish that."

All of Duff's brothers returned from the war, but only Angus, the second-youngest son, came back to the paper. Besides disrupting families and businesses, World War II brought other changes. The printing business was no exception. Newspapers across the country were going from letterpress, printing directly from type, to offset, which was printing on photo-etched aluminum plates and on roll-fed presses.

"Working with letterpress machinery was a risky business," Duff said. "It involved setting type with hot lead, and all of us have scars from it. Angus has burn scars where the hot lead squirted up his arm. I almost cut a finger off. My father lost a finger, my brother's hand was crushed and my sister, Harriet, lost the tip of the third finger on her left hand. 'But that's my wedding finger,' she said. She was seventeen years old at the time."

The Greens realized that they had to keep up with technology so they purchased a $500,000 offset press. In order to pay for it, they needed to find more work, which involved more debt as they purchased the *Madison County Eagle*, the *Greene County Record* and the *Rappahannock County News*.

Additionally, they were printing the *Louisa County Central Virginian* and the *Charlottesville-Albemarle Tribune*, several weekly newspapers in Maryland, and numerous other periodicals, as well as doing job printing. It was during this period that the name of the *Orange Review* was changed to the *Orange County Review*.

In the late 1960s, they incorporated into Green Publishers, with four offices in four counties and a payroll of more than fifty employees. They expanded into Orange, growing into another building and then another until they had eight adjacent structures in which to work.

The family joined forces again and went into overdrive. James W. Green Jr. had returned from his retirement in New England with his son, Ned. Duff had rejoined the business after returning from active duty with the Marine Corps, and his wife, Mary, not only taught school but also served as a part-time writer. Sister Lillian continued at her job, which she had held through the war, and another sister, Nancy, returned from northern Virginia with her husband, who also was a newspaperman with the *Washington Evening Star*, and they both joined the staff.

"At one time during the 1970s," says Duff, "there were more than a dozen adults and children, all named Green, who were setting type, running the presses, writing, taking photos, running the business office, sweeping the floor and cleaning the bathrooms."

He remembered having come back from being called to active duty with the marines for the Korean War, finishing his senior year at the University of Virginia and completing a year of law school until his GI Bill ran out, whereupon he returned to work at the paper.

Duff continued: "I showed up for work the first morning, and said, 'Dad, what do you want me to do?' He handed me a broom and said, 'Sweep the front walk.' 'But Dad, I have a college degree!' 'Oh, I forgot that,' said Dad. 'Give me the broom, I'll show you how.'"

Duff and his brother, Angus, became owners of the paper in 1965 when their father died, and when Angus was warned by his doctor to get away from the stress of the business, they accepted the offer of a conglomerate and sold the business in 1982.

Duff remained on staff at the *Orange County Review* as a writer and photographer until 1995, along with his sister, Lillian, who retired in 2002 after nearly sixty years with the paper. Duff couldn't stay away entirely, though, and continued to function as a news writer and photographer for the paper, as well as a writer for a weekly historical photo feature.

Orange County Tragedies

In January 1965, there was an enormous railroad accident in the town of Orange. A freight train came through loaded with steel trusses that were being sent on flatcars from Besom, Alabama, to New York State to build a school. They weren't loaded well, and the train was going a little too fast as it came around the curve at the edge of town. Centrifugal force broke the braces, the trusses started to fall between the wheels and the train derailed. The engine was pretty far down the track by then and took a while to stop. By that time, the trusses were going everywhere. One went completely through the train station and came out the other side. People were running every direction, and there were many close calls. One young mother with her baby in the car had stopped at the crossing and watched in horror as a truss slid toward the car, stopping just inches from its front wheels. It's a miracle that no one was hurt, although the brakeman in the caboose died of a heart attack.

Another memorable train accident happened just outside of the town on July 12, 1888, at what was known as the Fat Nancy Trestle, a landmark named after a very large African American woman who lived at the edge of town and always came out of her cabin door to wave at the passing trains. She was a favorite with the train crews, and they always looked for her and blew the whistle for her.

JJ ▽ 3
WRECK AT THE
FAT NANCY

Here, on 12 July 1888, occurred one of Virginia's
largest train disasters, the wreck of the Virginia
Midland Railroad's Train 52, the Piedmont Airline.
As it crossed the 44-foot-high, 467-foot-long
trestle, called the Fat Nancy for a local African
American woman who served as a trestle watcher
and reported problems, the trestle collapsed.
Nine passengers were killed, including two confederate veterans, and more than two dozen were
injured. Also killed was civil engineer Cornelius G.
Cox, who had earlier designed the current culvert
and earthen fill to replace the unstable trestle.
Former Confederate Lt. Gen. James Longstreet,
another passenger, survived.

The Fat Nancy trestle site is behind the historical marker designating the tragic event.

The accident happened after the commemoration of the twenty-fifth anniversary of the Battle of Gettysburg, which had taken place on July 4–5, 1863. A trainload of veterans, including General Longstreet, was going home heading south through Orange. They were going slow over the Fat Nancy Trestle when it collapsed at 4:00 a.m. Dozens were injured and eleven people died. General Longstreet spent several days in Orange as a guest at Meadowfarm before heading onward. The incident is still known as the worst train disaster in Virginia. Looters helped clean up the wreckage, and many local people have souvenirs. A brass rod from the baggage rack is in the James Madison Museum collection.

It is ironic that there were plans to make a fill at the trestle site. The construction engineer for the job, Cornelius Cox, had just boarded the train in Orange and lost his life in the accident. The keystone on a conduit at the site of the fill at Poplar Creek Run is dedicated to his memory.

Another major drama happened on November 8, 1908, when the town caught fire. Church bells frantically clanging in the early morning woke residents to the smell of smoke and cries of alarm. A wind-swept fire was spreading from Railroad Avenue through most of the town's business district, jumping the railroad tracks, destroying the station and continuing east to Byrd Street.

Two days later, ruins of buildings were still smoldering, including the skeleton of the Orange Baptist Church on the corner of East Main and Byrd Streets, where the 7-Eleven is located today. Adding to the tragedy is the fact that the church had just installed an expensive new pipe organ that was scheduled to play for the first time that Sunday morning. The cause of the fire was not a mystery, since Confederate veteran Towels Terrell admitted that he had started it.

Mr. Terrell, who preferred to be called "Colonel," was a colorful character whom townspeople looked on as their local philosopher. He was an educated man who carried the history of Orange County—and the world—in his head. He lived alone in an apartment over Ricketts Drug Store, which was located on Railroad Avenue in 1908. His income

Train station, Orange.

was a small salary for teaching in a one-room African American school at Nasons—he walked there, nine miles from Orange, every day. His one bad habit was smoking, which he said he started as a seventeen-year-old soldier in the Confederate army. He recalled that he was reading a newspaper when he fell asleep with a pipe or cigar or cigarette (records don't show which) in his hand. He would have burned to death had it not been for the night policeman who pulled him out of the flames.

George Lewis,
Grandson of Slaves

B orn and raised in Orange County, George Lewis had a long and lucrative career as a horticulturist in California and came back to "the home place" to spend his final years.

His grandfather, Chester Lewis, was owned by Bill Morton, who had a large number of slaves. During the Civil War, while Morton was away, he charged Chester with the safekeeping of the gold-plated table flatwear. Afraid to leave it untended during the day, Chester built a small compartment into the bottom of a hay wagon for it and then filled the wagon with hay to take to the cattle. At night, he hid it in a haystack. It's easy to imagine his nervous tension when Northern troops came into the area, but the family recalls that he remembered that they always spoke to him in a friendly way and, fortunately, did not find the flatwear.

When the Emancipation Proclamation took effect, the largest slave owner in the area was Dr. Mason, who owned large tracts on both sides of today's U.S. 522, off State Route 20. He deeded eighteen acres to his carriage man, Robert Ellis, known as "Punch," and said that he would sell adjoining acreage to Ellis's friends so that they all could be together. After the people heard the words, "You are free" at the local store, the Ellis, Lewis, Lindsay, Chapman, Chandler, Hall, Towles and Quarles families, with a total of some thirty children, settled in the community that they named Freetown to raise corn, hay and cattle.

George Lewis.

In rural areas, the population was predominantly black, and there were many opportunities for people to become acquainted. Wagons brought work parties to the various farms during harvest and haying seasons. After the first frost in the fall, which would eliminate most of the flies, hog-killing time was another important occasion—beginning at 4:00 a.m., it involved the slaughter of probably a dozen or more hogs.

Huge tubs of hot water scalded the carcasses, and then they were hung up overnight. The next day, the butchering began. Hams were covered with a mixture including salt, pepper, brown sugar and saltpeter for six weeks and then put in a smokehouse over a slow fire of hickory or fruit tree fuel to further dry the moisture from the meat in order to preserve it.

Summer revival meetings were also eagerly anticipated. Meetings went on all week and culminated with dinner on the grounds of the Bethel Baptist Church on the second Sunday in August and at Mount Pleasant Baptist on the fourth Sunday. Boards were nailed from tree to tree (some of which are there still) for the feasting, a time when the area's many good cooks had a chance to show their skills.

Another extremely popular August activity was the famed Orange Colored Horse Show, which flourished during the Great Depression. It began with a racing oval and show ring built by Lewis Ellis and his two sons, Gus and Marshall, on his property near Meadowfarm on State Route 612. It was an offshoot of the Orange Horse Show, a Triple-A event licensed by the American Horse Show Association that reflected the strong local interest in fine horses and horsemanship.

Ellis teamed up with others to form a corporation that issued stock in the operation, and by 1919 it had become an annual event that drew homeward local people who had migrated out of the area.

Interest in racing took precedence over horse showing, however, and mules also took part in some of the contests, which included flat track and sulky races, as well as jumping contests. Nobody wanted to win the prize for one of the mule races, however, as it was given to the last-place contestant. Loving cups and show ribbons were awarded along with lesser prizes that might include sacks of flour or meal or an automobile tire.

A few autos would be seen in the parking area along with a variety of carriages and wagons. There was a happy carnival atmosphere with a Ferris wheel, hot dogs, hamburgers, soft drinks, picnicking, the greeting of old friends and relatives and lots of flirting. Timely tips for a person's love life could be had from a phrenologist or a palm reader.

It was after dark, though, when the fun really went on. Bands like Kid Rainey's Trio from Richmond and the Honey Drippers, who also appeared at the Apollo Theater in New York, played far into the night for jitterbugs under bright lights on the dance floor that was located under the grandstand. By World War II, however, those lights had to go out, as blackout restrictions were imposed; sadly, those years also saw the end of the Orange Colored Horse Show.

"Freetown was a happy place. We had fun there. And it was picturesque," recalled George. "Long lanes with fences for horses and cattle, corn eight to ten feet tall and lots of apple and peach trees. Everyone had chickens, a cow or two, a horse that might be hitched to a plow during the week and to a buggy to go to town on Saturday and church on Sunday. The houses mostly were made of logs, sealed with a mixture of cement and lime and with lath and plaster on the inside. They were nice and warm in the winter, with a wood stove and fireplace, both of which were used for cooking."

George continued: "We hunted deer and rabbits, trapped fox and mink for pelts. We packed melon in straw, and kept at an even temperature, we could have them until Christmas. We picked gallons of wild grapes and berries for jams, jellies and wine. A slice of cake and a small glass of wine were enjoyed in the evenings. Blackberry and elderberry wine also were medicinal, and we made beer from persimmons."

Persimmons are one of Lewis's favorites. He gave the formal Latin horticultural name, *Diospyros virginiana*, "food of the gods," and agreed with that terminology.

All of the family members had their duties. "I used to dry five bushels of apples every year," said Lewis. "They were peeled and sliced, and I spread them on paper in the sun on the roof of a shed for a week. I had to take them up before night to keep off rain and dew. They were stored in gallon crockery jars or hung up in white cloth bags. Mother would make them into pies and on winter mornings boil two cups of dried apples in water for ten minutes to make delicious apple sauce."

Grandfather Chester Lewis believed strongly in education, and since there was no school for black children in the area, he built a twelve-by thirty-foot addition to his house for that purpose. George Lewis's aunt on his mother's side had married a Jamaican, Robert Stubbs, a former teacher, and he schooled thirty to forty children, each of whom contributed one dollar per month toward his salary.

The children walked to school, some as far as seven miles. George lived two miles from school and attended there for eleven years. Some of Stubbs's students went on to lead professional lives as lawyers and doctors.

By 1928, there was a segregated county elementary school, and seven years later, Elizabeth Lightfoot founded a high school for the black students. After integration, the children attended Lightfoot Elementary School in Unionville.

Over the years, and especially during wartime, many Freetown people migrated north for better jobs and for the opportunity to own their own homes. Several of the women, relying on their cooking skills, found positions with wealthy families in New York, Philadelphia and Baltimore.

Some of the men went with their families to the Pennsylvania coal mines and steel mills.

Lewis's sister, Edna, became a well-known cook. She started at a hotel in Washington and then went to New York, where she had her own restaurant, and she eventually started a cooking school in Atlanta. A frequent guest on TV talk shows, she produced several elegant cookbooks, the last of which, *The Gift of Southern Cooking*, was published in 2003.

Pearline Ellis, a Freetown acquaintance of Lewis, was encouraged by her friend, Matt Henson, an envoy to Admiral Robert Perry, to go even farther afield to Alaska to trap for furs, which she brought annually to an uncle in New York who had business connections with furriers. She ultimately took her earnings to California and became active in real estate in the Los Angeles area. A millionaire when she died, she was known as a generous philanthropist.

In the meantime, said George, "I was working as a field hand for fifty cents a day and [was] in the Civilian Conservation Corps until World War II. The war was a turning point. I was drafted and went to Frankfurt, Germany, where I was a corporal in the medical corps."

He took advantage of the GI Bill when he was discharged in 1946, earning a bachelor's degree in horticulture from Hampton College and later doing graduate work in entomology.

What made him choose to go to California? "I met a girl," he said simply. How many destinies are determined by those four words?

It was a happy destiny for George and his wife, Hortense. He became the director of La Canada, an eighty-acre botanical garden and arboretum near Los Angeles where he supervised a permanent crew of twenty-five plus a large number of volunteer workers. He grew the roses for the Pasadena Rose Parade, for which he was a float decorator, and after he retired, the city flew him back to conduct Christmas decoration workshops.

He retired after thirty-three years, and since Hortense had died and they had no children, he returned to the Freetown area, where he had relatives, and built a beautiful home.

Orange County did not present the opportunity to be idle, however, and his talents were graciously and freely given to, and greatly appreciated by, the town of Orange. Multiple flower beds

George Lewis memorial plaque, Orange.

and planters still give testimony to his skill and generosity. He was a popular speaker at garden clubs and offered his skills as a landscape designer. He also was active in the Baptist Center in Rixeyville, where he helped with fundraising, landscaping and construction.

George died in 2007. A memorial in one of his gardens on Madison Road at Main Street in Orange is a tribute to his dedication and skills. He will not be forgotten.

Railroad Avenue

The Little Street that Was

He had a brand new Graphic Graflex press camera in his hand and just had to take a picture—any picture.

When Duff Green stepped outside the *Orange Review* newspaper office in the fall of 1956, he looked along the street at the row of businesses on Railroad Avenue that faced the train tracks. He stood on the tracks, put the camera up and called across to some friends socializing along the sidewalk: "Hey, try to look like you have good sense." They laughed and joked back at him, and he snapped the picture, documenting the busiest street in town, only one block long, that was the heart of the town of Orange for almost one hundred years.

Railroad Avenue runs north and south between Main Street and Church Street. Duff related that it had its start with the completion of the Orange and Alexandria Railroad in 1854, when commercial businesses began to be established there, across the tracks from the passenger station built near where the county jail had existed in the late 1700s.

The area came into prominence after the Battle of Gettysburg in July 1863 when, during the following winter, thousands of Lee's Confederate soldiers were located in the area, encamped for miles along the Rapidan River. The railroad passenger and freight stations were filled with hay, grain and military supplies as trains packed with more supplies—as well as troops, including the wounded—rolled in and out of town.

Duff Green with a Railroad Avenue picture.

After the war, both freight and passenger services became well established, and passengers could get off the trains and find a meal or shopping opportunities while awaiting connections or while engines refueled with coal and water. Freight and mail were transferred at the little station, still in place, near where C.R. Butler's hardware store building stands. Those tracks still exist, although they have been removed where they crossed Byrd Street.

By the 1920s, the commercial property along Railroad Avenue had become the most valuable real estate in town. Through the years, of course, the properties changed ownership, and some shifted locations. Grymes Drug Store, for instance, was established there in the 1890s and was destroyed in a devastating fire on November 8, 1908. It was relocated in 1909 to West Main Street, and about ten years later, it was moved again, to East Main Street, to the left of the present location of the arts center. It reached its present location on West Main Street in the 1980s.

At different times, Railroad Avenue had restaurants, pool halls, livery stables and corrals, the Morris Hotel, the Sunny South Grocery Store, the Sanitary Grocery—whose name still can be seen painted on the brick—a dance hall, barbershops, several saloons (including the famous, or infamous, 'Nuff Said Saloon) and Fink's Five and Ten Cent Store.

Fink was an enterprising mountaineer who started a moonshine business during prohibition and made so much money that after repeal he "went legit," as Duff said. Fink opened his store on Railroad Avenue and built a fine house in town.

Next door to the store was the busy Railroad Express Agency. When the building was taken down, the REA signs were pulled from the front, and Duff took one off the truck as it was headed for the landfill. It now sits over the fireplace in his den, disdaining the $100 he was offered for it at the time.

One of the area's largest dry goods stores, Levy's, was started in the 1890s by Emil Levy, who had originally stepped off the train a few yards away and found his niche on Railroad Avenue. Like the other structures on the east end of town, the store and the station were destroyed in the 1908 fire. Two years later, Levy had built the store back up, better than ever. The structure, built in what was then an ultramodern style, still stands on the corner of Railroad and Main Streets.

Railroad Avenue flourished between 1854 and the 1950s until the trucking industry began to carry freight and train passengers began to use automobiles. As the train station gradually declined in use, the establishments along Railroad Avenue began to lose customers, and businesses moved westward down Main Street, to Madison Road and to Chapman Street. The *Orange Review* newspaper gobbled up eight spaces in the area, and other businesses were established along the railroad tracks as real estate prices declined there.

Recent renovations and new owners of the sturdy brick buildings brought a new look to Railroad Avenue in the early 2000s; it had stood neglected for so long, "the little street that still is."

Brimstone? No. Fire? Definitely

You have to say this for the Orange Baptists: they never give up. After being burned out twice, and also given the fire that destroyed their parsonage, they bravely carry on tradition today in their third brick building on Main Street in Orange. They commemorated their 150th anniversary there in 2006.

The congregation had its beginning at Zion Baptist Church, located "out in the country" about three miles south of the town, that was known then as Orange Court House until it was chartered in 1892 and described as "a thriving village, surrounded by a wealthy, refined and intelligent population."

A church history indicates that records of Zion Church for June 19, 1858, show that twelve members applied for letters of dismissal, meaning that they were removing their names as members of that congregation. The remaining members of the Zion congregation built another church five miles from Orange toward Gordonsville.

The group that moved into Orange was made up of both men and women whose names were Aikens, Beadles, Boulevare, Newman, Quarles, Rawlings and Scott, one of whom was thought to be an African American since both slaves and freed people worshiped together with whites in the congregation.

Dr. Charles Quarles, a former medical doctor turned pastor, headed the committee of charter members to organize the move. As can be expected after all of the fires, early dates are hard to establish, but county records show that Dr. Quarles, Thomas Scott and Benjamin Rawlings made up the "Orange Court House Church trustees" who, on October 14, 1856, purchased a seventy-four-square-foot plot behind the courthouse from Richard Rawlings and his wife, Lucy, for one dollar. The location is shown on a Confederate military map.

This first building, begun in 1856, measured thirty-eight by fifty-five feet and included a vestibule, a steeple and a basement room, stabilized with "a good stock brick" on one side and at the end of the structure. It was to cost $2,900, not including painting. Construction began in 1856, and the first service was held there two years later. It was destroyed by fire in April 1871. The cornerstone of that building, laid by members of the local Masonic Lodge chapter, is now incorporated into the wall of the current church's lobby.

Following the fire, the land was sold to the county for $180, and the courthouse building was expanded onto the site to incorporate a jail. The congregation migrated down Main Street to a location about one hundred feet east of the railroad tracks and purchased land from E.W. Row for $400.

Two years later, in 1873, the site held an elegant new building with an octagonal Italianate cupola, slender spires on each corner of the building and pointed arches above the front door.

Saint Thomas Church

In a county as old as Orange, it's quite a distinction to be the oldest church, although Saint Thomas, in the town of Orange, had to start out Anglican in order to do it. Since so much of the history of the area starts during the time of Governor Spottswood, that's a natural place to begin when telling the church's story.

Alexander Spottswood was governor of Virginia from 1710 to 1722. When he first took definitive steps to move colonization westward and establish the legendary Germanna iron mine, Orange County and what became Saint Thomas Parish were part of Spotsylvania County and St. Mark's Parish. Over a number of succeeding years, the amoeba-like shifting boundaries of both resulted in Orange County's founding in 1734 and the designation of Saint Thomas Parish in 1740, its western limit at that point being the summit of the Blue Ridge Mountains.

Since church records before 1852 were destroyed during the Civil War, the story of Saint Thomas depends on information from a history of the church written in 1933, as well as from an earlier series of two books written by Bishop Meade and titled *Old Churches, Ministers and Families of Virginia*. The sections on Saint Thomas rely heavily on the contributions of Reverend Joseph Earnest, then its rector, written in 1857.

Reverend Earnest described the first church, called Church in the Wilderness, as being built "about 10 miles northwest of Orange Court

House on the right bank of the Rapidan River" near an ancient Indian burial ground.

He indicated that he was told the church was used as early as 1723 and that it was still in use in 1740. The minister at that time was a Scot, "whose name I have not been able to ascertain but who it seems was fond of good cheer and a game of cards."

Eventually, the church was moved about eight miles closer to the developing center of county population, where it still was standing in 1857.

Saint Thomas Parish had three more structures before the Revolutionary War; the oldest of these was called the Orange Church, situated near Ruckersville; the Pine Stake Church; and, appropriately, the Middle or Brick Church, located between the other two. Earnest stopped to see it one day and described it this way: "The old church, which is of wood, has undergone so many repairs since the time it was built, that...little of any of the original timber is to be found in it. As I passed it...my heart was saddened to see this relic of former times so far gone into dilapidation as to be wholly unfit for the sacred purposes for which it was set apart."

The structure that was known as the Middle or Brick Church fared better structurally, at least initially. It was located on land owned by the Taylor family about three miles northeast of Orange Court House on Fredericksburg Road, on the property now known as Meadowfarm. It was thought to have been built between 1750 and 1758, and by 1806 it was still in good condition.

"But," said Reverend Earnest, "what time failed to accomplish was reached by the unsparing hand of man" when usable building materials were taken away. "The walls fell, and the triumph of the invaders was complete, as they carried away so many captives, the vanquished, unresisting bricks. The altar-pieces, executed in gilt letters...were torn from their ancient resting-places, went into fragments, and were afterward attached to some articles of household furniture."

Fortunately, the massive silver cup and paten used for communion were saved. Engraved with Saint Thomas's name, Earnest estimated that they had been donated about a century before by Mrs. Frances Madison, grandmother of President James Madison; Mrs. James Taylor; Mrs.

Balmaine; "and other good women." They are used now at Christmas and Easter services.

The exact year in which the last of the ancient trio, Pine Stake Church, was built is also lost. It had stood on land originally owned by Francis Taliafero near Mountain Run, about fifteen miles northeast of Orange Court House. It still was standing as late as 1813.

From about 1800 into the 1830s, parishioners met in one another's homes or in the county courthouse. Ministers of different faiths often donated their services, including Presbyterian James Waddell, the famed "Blind Preacher," whose little wooden church was located a few miles south of town.

Finally the congregation was able to purchase a lot from James Forbes on Caroline Street, where the present building was begun in 1833. It was patterned after Christ Church in Charlottesville, purported to be the only religious structure ever drawn by Jefferson. It is possible that part of the work was done by slaves owned by parishioners.

Reverend Earnest candidly reported that during the 1850s, heated discussions over the nonpayment of his salary twice resulted in his resignation. Eventually, times improved, ministers were paid and a new front to the building was added in the 1850s, with columns that support the steeple coming at a later date.

In addition to the treasure of the communion silver, favorite historic mementos include the pew in which Lee sat during services the winter of 1863–64 and the locust tree in the front of the building, which has its own plaque on the adjacent wall designating it as the place where his horse, Traveler, waited for him.

One memorable day was Sunday, November 22, 1863, when both Jefferson Davis and Lee attended church. Captain Benjamin Wesley, justice of North Carolina, reported in a letter written to his wife that he "arrived early to secure good seats." He described Davis as being the "lean, intellectual President" and referred to Lee at one point as "beefy and fat" yet holding "a high head and is the very impersonation of dignity and manly power."

After hard times during and after the war, by 1885 the vestry was able to make further improvements to the church building. Rectangular window frames were replaced with arches and stained-glass panes, one of which was made in the Tiffany workrooms. A small parish hall was constructed in 1912, as well as the present one in 1928.

In the 1920s, members voted whether to follow the trend in the South of trying to erase memories of slavery by removing church galleries that traditionally had been used by slaves. There was only one vote against the action at Saint Thomas; the narrow winding stair and balcony were taken away.

Additions since 1962 include the rector's study, the brick walks, the covered and enclosed entrances and a large parking lot behind the church. The rector's study alone came at a cost of $85,000, in comparison to the $3,350 cost of building the original church in 1833.

The church also has the unusual distinction of having been awarded recognition by both the U.S. Department of Interior and the Virginian Historic Landmarks Commission, but its spirit can best be described by another quote, still apropos, from Reverend Earnest: "Saint Thomas was to feel the effects of war and panics, struggling along through prosperity and hard times, and now…we find a church complete in all its details, ready to serve its members and the world, in all ways."

The Silk Mill of Orange

He told me, 'They treated me so nicely I just couldn't tell them 'No,''" said Duff Green, remembering a newspaper interview he had in the late 1950s with Milton Reuben, the son of the owner of the American Silk Mills, with locations in New York, New Jersey and Pennsylvania.

The time was 1928, and labor costs for workers in northern states had become expensive. An ad in the *Wall Street Journal* for a mill site in the South had caught the eye of Carol Slaughter, founder and president of the Citizen's National Bank in Orange. Well aware of the need for industry in Orange County, Slaughter, on behalf of the chamber of commerce, responded to the advertisement that ultimately brought Milton Reuben to the train station on Main Street.

Slaughter and a delegation from the chamber of commerce met Reuben as he stepped off the train, and a parade of brightly shined autos made a procession down Main Street to the new James Madison Hotel, where they had lunch. Southern hospitality worked its wiles on the silk mill heir, and six months later, an electric-powered modern brick and glass building erected for about $250,000 was located on North Madison Road.

"You have to remember what Orange was like in those days," said Duff. "Many streets were unpaved. There was limited electrical power, no public sewer system, the halfway water system dating from 1910 was antiquated and the population of the town was maybe 1,500 people.

The only industry was Kentucky Flooring Company, and the rest was agriculture." In order to accommodate the new mill, the town council was forced to put in a sewer system. ("I should have asked," said Reuben later.)

There were virtually no nonfarm jobs for women in Orange's agrarian landscape. Farm women worked long, hard hours, and when the Great Depression settled in, cash money went from scarce to practically nonexistent. An ad in the *Orange Review* asking for women age sixteen years and above to work in a clean environment with good working conditions and good pay drew many a farm girl, as well as her female relatives and friends, all eager to receive up to fifteen dollars every other Saturday for a sixty-hour workweek.

Reuben offered every member of the Orange High School's graduating class of 1928 a job. All except one young man accepted the offer. The mill also offered an annual college scholarship.

"I never made so much money in my life," Edna Harlow Tucker told Duff years later, remembering those days. "I didn't know what I was going to do with it. I secretly bought a cream separator as a surprise for my father. It was the only time I ever saw him cry."

"Management came from other Reuben mills," said Duff, "and a team of people arrived in Orange to set up and train a few local men to maintain the machines, do the cleaning and whatnot, along with a crew of five women from Lancaster, Pennsylvania, to teach women the weaving trade. Most of the workers were women because they had small hands. They had to work at the spinning machines and in the warp and weft of the weaving machines."

Huge oval-shaped bales of unbelievably expensive silk from China and Japan would come to the train station, wrapped in burlap. They were so valuable that a steel vault was built at the mill to store them.

Silk fiber is both extremely fine and strong. The single fibers from the bales had to be put onto spools and then spun—twisted together—in doubling and quadrupling machines to make a four-strand thread that could be woven into usable fabric. Each worker wore an apron and had a little pair of scissors attached to her belt. When one of the silk strands broke, she would very delicately tie the pieces together and carefully snip off the ends of the knot, making it nearly invisible.

"Rueben would make periodic inspection trips to Orange," Duff recalled with a smile, "to be met at the train by his chauffer and driven to Gaston Hall, the home he purchased on Montpelier Road. The mill workers had a code to let them know he was in the area, and everything was quickly put in readiness for him. He insisted that everything be spotlessly clean. Reuben told me that he saw one of the men busily sweeping up one day, and he said, 'Young man, do you always work this hard?' Not recognizing the owner, the man said, 'No, just when that s.o.b. Reuben is here!'"

Duff continued: "Working at the mill provided the best life and the most fun a lot of people had. Buses brought workers from Culpeper, Madison, Greene and Louisa Counties. They marched in parades, had Sunday afternoon picnics and a big annual picnic at Fairview Beach on the Potomac River near Fredericksburg. They enjoyed a very strong camaraderie."

The women in Orange eventually outproduced the work done in both the New York and Pennsylvania plants. When the New York mills closed, their business was sent to Orange, providing even more opportunity, and the mill escalated in size, spreading along North Madison Road. In its heyday, the only silk mill in the world larger than the one in Orange was in Japan.

The workers and the town adjusted to the opportunities and changes they brought. Stores opened and businesses thrived, including the *Orange Review*, owned by the Green family.

"Although some people complained that changes were 'ruining Orange,'" said Duff, "during the Depression and especially at the time of World War II, the mill supported the local economy. Good times flowed. Suddenly, women had become breadwinners, and they achieved bank loans to buy or build homes, based on their salaries."

Duff continued: "World War II really was the kicker, though, and the reason was parachutes. More than a thousand workers, again mostly women,—they called themselves 'silk worms'—worked three eight-hour shifts to produce the most parachutes in the country. The silk had been coming first from China, and then from Japan until December 7, 1941. Suddenly there was no shipping and so no source of supply. The mill had to switch to synthetic fabrics like nylon, rayon or Dacron."

The new fibers were heavier, and it was hard to adjust the machines to deal with them. In about 1960, the aging Milton Reuben sold the Orange mill, and production declined. New machinery in New York and New Jersey mills outperformed the one in Orange; after sixty years, it was closed.

Today, businesses of many types have space in the old silk mill buildings. It is fascinating to look at the glossy floors and see stains and patches where machinery was located that did who knows what. Some businesses have installed dropped ceilings, but in others, pipes and pulleys remain, indicating the arcane mysteries of silk production that gave Orange a major place in the manufacturing world, along with events and tales that local people still enjoy remembering.

Holladay House

S am and Sharon Elswick sat in their warm, inviting parlor overlooking
Main Street in Orange, surrounded by furnishings and architectural
elements either dating to or reflecting the period and history of their
home and business.

"We are the third owners of the Holladay House Bed-and-Breakfast
that was started here by Pete and Phebe Holladay in 1989," said
Sharon. "Many of the furnishings we use were theirs. The history of
the house goes back 180 years, and it often has been used as a business
as well as a residence." Fireplace surrounds, floors and chair rails—as
well as windows, with their exterior plastered brick lintels—remain
intact. The only architectural changes made were those necessary for
the B&B business.

An elegant wraparound porch, roofed on the street side, was added
by the Holladay family early in the twentieth century. However, the steps
and porch section along the front of the house had to be removed when
Main Street was widened by the Works Progress Administration (WPA)
in 1934. "The remaining side porch was restored by Pete Holladay, using
much of the existing materials and keeping it as close to the original as
possible," said Sharon.

The story of the Holladay House begins in the 1830s when Hugh
Stevens purchased property from Paul Verdier, who had bought part

Holladay House. *Courtesy of Sam Elswick.*

of the William Bell farm in the growing settlement then called Orange Court House in 1799. Stevens constructed his brick two-story Federal-style house, consisting of a central hall with two rooms down and two above, over an English basement.

The residence passed from Stevens through the Page and Willis families to a grand-nephew of President James Madison, John Madison Chapman, in 1849. "Chapman was a lawyer," said Sam. "His law office was in the house, and he had served as the town's mayor."

At one point during the Civil War, there was a cavalry skirmish between the two armies along Main Street, which then was only about twelve feet wide. Legend has it that a Confederate soldier died on the front steps.

The Chapmans had eight children, only one of whom was a son. The two eldest daughters, Emma and Mary, married lieutenants in the Confederate army. "A military medical tent was set up across the street," said Sam, "and Carol Couch, president of the historical society, has a copy of an 1864 diary from a Dr. Apperson there." Apperson felt that the daughters were socially condescending to him, but he accepted an invitation to Emma's wedding that also was attended by Generals Stuart, Rhodes, Chilton and Perry.

"Chapman went into debt," said Sam, "and a chancery suit with a general store owner led to his financial ruin. After his death, his wife was forced to sell. The McDonald family bought it in 1883, including the lot next door where the Corner House Gallery is now, which at one time served as the parsonage for the Methodist church."

Dr. Lewis Holladay acquired the property in 1899, and the family owned it for 101 years, more than enough time to give permanency to the name of Holladay House. There were six children in the family, three daughters and three sons, two of whom were twins, resulting in the house being expanded toward the rear of the property.

Traditionally, the right side of the house, now living quarters for the Elswicks, was leased for businesses, and Dr. Lewis Holladay had his medical practice there. His son, Pete, remembered, as a child, daring to open the forbidden closet door where a human skeleton was hanging, jabbing a finger out to touch it and recoiling in horror.

One daughter, Aubrey, remembered as being a good athlete on the Orange High School baseball and basketball teams, also assisted her father at birthings. Dr. Holladay's sister, Louise, also lived in the house. She was a teacher and her brother built a small one-room schoolhouse for her use beside their home. When that section of the property was sold for a building lot, the schoolhouse was moved to the rear of the property.

Pete and Phebe inherited the house and in 1989 turned it into a bed-and-breakfast inn. The next owner, Judy Geary, continued the business, and in 2006 Sharon and Sam moved to Orange to be the new owners and managers of the property.

A reception honoring the twentieth anniversary of the bed-and-breakfast business was held in November 2009, filling the house with people who brought memories of the family and those who either lived or did business there. One gentleman recalled that Dr. Holladay, who performed physical examinations for both World Wars I and II, "gave me a clean bill of health and sent me off to war."

Dentists also leased space, and Orange's mayor, Henry Lee Carter, wondered if a circular mark in the floor where his law office once was located might have been where the chair was located. He also noted that Dr. Chewning was known for not using Novocain, resulting in his being referred to as "Dr. Pain."

Sharon grew up in New Jersey, and Sam's family is originally from Virginia. His archaeology degree from the College of William and Mary sent him into the backyard to find nineteenth-century ceramics and glass, nails and a small medical bottle. Time allowing, further exploration is planned that will add more artifacts to the information and items already archived in their collection of Holladay House memorabilia.

Mayhurst Inn

Jack North interrupted his duty of polishing his wife Pat's notable collection of silver teaspoons to talk about Mayhurst, their elegant Victorian home, one of Orange County's fine bed-and-breakfast inns.

"John Willis built Mayhurst in 1859 for his wife, Lucy, and eight children," he said. "The property consisted of 2,800 acres. He was a great-nephew of James Madison and had grown up on the Montpelier plantation." Willis was a circuit court judge, a well-to-do plantation owner and the founder of the Orange and Alexandria Railroad.

In 1829, the property was known as the Howard place, and several buildings original to the site still are there, including the one-room schoolhouse built in 1837 now used for guest space, as well as the original plantation house that later became the summer kitchen, with space above in which the house slaves slept.

Mayhurst's Italianate Victorian style, the height of architectural fashion at the time, is echoed in the county courthouse on Main Street in Orange, also built in the late 1850s but on a less flamboyantly elegant scale. Its architect, Norris G. Stackweather of Baltimore, may also have drawn plans for Willis's home, thought to be the second- or third-largest house in Orange County at the time.

Mayhurst has about 9,200 square feet of space, twenty-two rooms (eight of them guest rooms) and seventeen shallow, coal-burning

Mayhurst.

fireplaces. All of the arches, floor-to-ceiling windows and extensive woodwork are original.

The elegant spiral staircase leads up three floors, with an extension to the cupola. "The staircase railing gets shorter going up," said Jack, "since the smallest of the Willis's eight children were on the third floor. Coming down, you notice that the steps slant three degrees toward the railing, making you want to hold on to it."

Once, during a wedding party, the Norths found guests' children dropping toys from the top of the staircase onto the cake, sitting on the table four levels below.

"John Willis was an ardent Confederate," said Jack, "and became a major contributor to the cause, unfortunately investing heavily in Confederate bonds. He was unable to pay his taxes after the war and lost at least 1,700 of the original nearly 3,000 acres, and Mayhurst was purchased by a Northerner sent by the government to act as an administrator to Orange County."

Mayhurst coal burning fireplace.

Mayhurst staircase.

As recorded in letters and biographies, Willis was generous with his hospitality. He hosted Generals A.P. Hill, Robert E. Lee, Stonewall Jackson and perhaps more not recorded. It was Hill's headquarters, and his headquarters tent was located under the big tree in the front yard from November 1863 to May 1864, the beginning of the Battle of the Wilderness.

One of General Hill's daughters was christened at Mayhurst on May 1, 1864, held by her godfather, General Robert E. Lee. A painting by contemporary artist Mort Kunstler marks the occasion, hanging in the family parlor where the ceremony took place.

Several Civil War events took place on the property. Probably the first, Jack recounted, was in early August 1862, just before the start of the Battle of Cedar Mountain. A Union cavalry unit had driven one of Jackson's units under General Jones out of the town. Many had gathered on Mayhurst's front lawn, and records note that one of the Willis girls,

Mayhurst baptism painting.

said to be "very comely," went out on the front porch and asked them to go back, join their command and "do their duty." A major whom Jones had sent over to rally the troops and bring them back arrived as she was making the statement; she added that she wished she was a man, at which point one of the men in the crowd said, "Missy, if you was a man, you would want to be a woman again mighty soon."

"I guess it worked," said Jack, "because they went back and drove the Yankees out of Orange."

About eighteen thousand troops were spread across the Mayhurst property when it was Hill's headquarters. "I don't think we've started to plant anything around here where we haven't dug up something," said Jack. "We let our guests use the metal detector, and most of them have found things—Minié balls, buttons, belt buckles—which they can take home as prized mementos."

The Norths have traced the property owners from 1859 to the present, and there have been a number of those family reunions at Mayhurst.

For the most part, the house was well cared for up until 1990, when it was abandoned for about six years. However, it was never vandalized, and although there was water damage, 90 percent of the glass is original, as is almost all of the woodwork and nearly all of the floors. The house basically is the way it was built. It was put on the National Register for Historic Places in 1985 and is also classed as a Virginia historical landmark.

Pat and Jack both grew up in Upstate New York, met at a college party, married in 1969 and became the parents of two girls and a boy. They lived outside Leesburg, and both worked in what Jack termed "the great corporate world of northern Virginia." Pat's career was in social work as an Alzheimer's/dementia specialist. Jack was the director of a national healthcare information company.

They decided that they wanted to escape. "The decision to own a B&B came about gradually," said Pat. One of their daughters was to be married in 2001, and they had looked at a lot of places for a wedding site, but where she really wanted was to be married was at Tara, the plantation from *Gone with the Wind*. They looked everywhere for another Tara for a long six months and found some places, some of them B&Bs,

but discovered that there were so many restrictions for using them that they thought it was ridiculous. "You couldn't really use the house or go inside except for photographing the wedding party," said Pat. "It was very frustrating. We jokingly said, 'We could do this.'"

They were both traveling a lot at the time, Jack all over the world and Pat along the East Coast. "In phone conversations between our motel rooms," she said, "after, 'What did you do today?' we'd get off on, 'If we had a home like that we'd let people use it. We'd let people enjoy it.' After several years, even after the wedding, I said, 'I really appreciate your playing the game with me, but I'm serious. I'd love to find an old home. And he said, 'I thought you were playing the game. *I'm* serious.'"

They spent about two and a half years trying to find a place, a piece of property to totally restore, and found Mayhurst, advertised as a thirty-seven-acre estate for sale. "We came up the drive," said Jack, "and decided it looked like a wedding cake on a hill. It fit. The Harmons were interested in selling; we were interested in buying."

Peg and Bob Harmon had already brought Mayhurst back from terrible shape and had operated it as a B&B since 1998. They come back about once a year to visit.

The Norths have pictures that the Harmons took of how it looked when they bought it "neglected, abandoned, just awful," but now it has everything that the Norths had wanted and talked about. Why would they spend two to three years making a home when the Harmons had already done it? The furnishings are mostly from the 1850s to 1860s, some of which they bought from the Harmons and the rest they had collected over time in anticipation of their goal. "I'm in heaven," said Pat.

"After all the looking, probably it was the easiest thing we did, to buy this house," said Jack. "It just clicked. The transition was easy. We have no regrets whatsoever. It's fun...And being in Orange County is so nice. Everybody is so welcoming and kind. When people around here say, 'Have a nice day,' they actually mean it."

The Norths say that estimates are that along with the other local B&Bs, about 30–35 percent of their guests are repeat visitors. They are awed by Mayhurst's architecture and its preservation. "They like its solitude, yet being so close to town. They are very impressed by what Orange has to

Mayhurst parlor.

offer—Montpelier, wineries, restaurants, the history, antiques, vistas and the terrain. They can be in northern Virginia and ninety minutes later be in another world. They come tensed up but by Saturday morning are relaxed, and on Sunday morning they want to stay," said Jack.

So what's in the future? "When we can't walk up these stairs anymore," said Pat, "we'll try to find someone with a commitment to preserving the property."

A Visit to Montpelier, 1827

Mr. Madison is quite a short thin man with his head bald except on the back, where his hair hangs down to his collar & over his ears, nicely powdered—he has gray but bright eyes, & small features—he looks scarcely as old as he is, 74, and seems very hale & hearty—the expression of his face is full of good humour."

Such were the observations of Henry D. Gilpin, a young Philadelphia lawyer, in a letter written to his father dated September 16, 1827. When he began the letter, he had traveled three hundred miles from home into Virginia, where he was very impressed that he was riding ten miles, alone, into Staunton on a borrowed horse and wondered what his "mother would be saying if she was aware of it." He went on to Lexington and was totally overwhelmed by Natural Bridge, which he thought was better than Niagara Falls. He provided nearly five pages of description, finding it "so deep & terrific that no one could once dare to approach the edge—you naturally & unconsciously throw yourself on your knees & creep to a precipice so tremendous that it is long before you can accustom your eye to look down for more than an instant."

Gilpin continued onward to visit Monticello, Charlottesville and the University of Virginia campus. He hired a carriage and left there at about 9:00 a.m., bound for Fredericksburg, sixty-five miles away, with a stop at Montpelier.

The front of Montpelier.

He came into Orange County "near Barboursville...close by two nobles houses, of the two Mr. Barbours—the Secretary of the Treasury & the gentleman who is talked of as the opposition speaker next winter—the brothers being of different politics."

He arrived at Montpelier "after a ride over hills, through woods, and long roads, where we had constantly to open gates—and often the adventure of a breakdown we reached there early in the afternoon... Mr. Madison's house is a very large one, with a noble portico in front and extensive wings on each side. When I arrived he & Mrs. Madison were out having gone over to a relation's in the neighborhood. I amused myself in examining the grounds around, & the room in which I was."

Gilpin waited in the entrance hall, where he could see views both to the front and back of the house. He looked to the back and saw "the lawn extending to the woods. The view in the front extends to the Blue mountain about 30 or 40 miles off & is a fine one though not so much as many I have seen of that picturesque ridge."

According to Gilpin:

Much of the furniture of the room had the appearance of Presidential splendour such a sofas covered with crimson damask on each side, three or four large looking glasses—& everything displayed in its arrangement with great order neatness and taste—for which I fancy Mrs. Madison is remarkable. There are some large & good historical pictures by Flemish artists; & several portraits around the walls—among the latter two excellent ones of Genl. Washington & Mr. Jefferson—a great number of busts—a bronze figure of Napoleon and some good casts of antique statues.

In a little while, a fine portly looking lady, with a straw bonnet, and shawl on came in which I once took for her ladyship & mentioned my name; she asked if I was any relation to you, & on saying I was your son, she expressed much pleasure at seeing me, asked a great deal after

Madison statues, Montpelier.

*you & my mother, said it would give Mr. Madison great gratification to
see me, and indeed treated me with the greatest kindness. Soon after Mr.
Madison came in & I gave him your & my other letter, while I went on
talking with Mrs. M. and Mrs. Cutts, her sister, who also asked much
after you, Philadelphia, & her old acquaintances.*

Gilpin continued his description of the president:

*He was dressed in black, with breeches & old fashioned top boots, which
he afterwards took off & sat during the evening in his white stockings,
but the next day he had black silk on & looked very nice.*

*Mrs. Madison slipped off to change her walking dress & made
herself quite stylish in a turban & fine gown—she has a great deal of
dignity blended with good humor & knowledge of the world. A number
of her relations were staying with them, a party I suppose of a dozen
& two or three pretty girls among them. The latter I fear will think me
a poor beau, for I scarcely spoke 20 words to them—the truth is pretty
girls I can find plenty of, but I could see but one Mr. Madison, &
probably never again.*

Gilpin and Madison stayed up late, and Gilpin remarked that "with the
exception of a little conversation now & then with Mrs. Madison—I talked
with or rather listened to him almost exclusively while I remained." The
president was full of good jokes and stories, and they spoke at length about
general politics and both ancient and modern literature.

Madison asked about the Delaware and Chesapeake Canal, which
would be completed two years later in 1829, that connects Chesapeake
Bay with the Atlantic. The project had long been a Gilpin family project.
It was first surveyed by a Thomas Gilpin in the 1760s, and was a major
interest of Joshua Gilpin, father of the letter writer, to whom the president
sent congratulations on its near completion.

Gilpin was down the next morning some time before the ladies
appeared, but not before Madison, whom he found reading in the parlor:
"He urged me to stay two or three days but I could not do so without
a good deal of inconvenience & expense in keeping the carriage I had

hired." He stayed some time after breakfast and prepared to continue his travels. "When I came off they desired their particular remembrance to you & my mother, & hope that you may be induced to pay them a visit, which they say you may do by a journey of but a few days. Mrs. M. desired her 'affectionate' remembrance to you which I suppose refers to old times, for she talked a great deal about them and her intimacy with my aunt."

The letter ended when he arrived in Fredericksburg, but he did not mail it there, instead sending it from Baltimore on September 19 with an addendum saying that his health was never better but that his wardrobe and pockets were rather poor. He asked that if his father would send him "ten or fifteen dollars," he would be able to meet his needs "and return the same with legal interest according to law on return to the city of brotherly love."

The Mothers Madison

The Montpelier property has been blessed with women who left their marks on it by stewardship, through marriage or through their children.

The first mother at Montpelier was Frances Taylor Madison, daughter of James Taylor, who was, among other things, a member of the Knights of the Golden Horseshoe and a surveyor for Spotsylvania County. In 1722, he patented 8,500 acres of land in what was to become Orange County and was additionally instrumental in securing 4,675 acres of jointly patented property for his two sons-in-law, Thomas Chew and Ambrose Madison.

Ambrose and Frances, who were married in 1721, called their 2,337½-acre property Mount Pleasant and moved there from Caroline County in 1732 with their three children: James, who would become father of our fourth president, and daughters Elizabeth and Frances. The property was developing nicely, with a main house and outbuildings, as well as farm buildings and a sizeable number of slaves, cattle, hogs, sheep and horses.

Tragically, Ambrose was only to survive for six months at Mount Pleasant. He died from being poisoned. Three slaves were involved in the crime. One, who did not belong to him, was executed, and the other two, who were Madison property, were punished and returned to the plantation.

Ambrose's will stipulated that the Mount Pleasant property was to go to Frances until their son, James, reached majority in 1741, but she had the legalities adjusted so that they co-operated the plantation until her death, on April 25, 1761. It was rare, at the time, that a wealthy widow did not remarry, but Frances, at age thirty-two, learned to manage Mount Pleasant at a profit and, in a few years, began marketing tobacco in England.

Her son James married Eleanor (Nelly) Rose Conway in September 1749. They lived at Mount Pleasant and started their family of twelve children, which included the firstborn, also named James, who was stillborn; Rueben, who died at age four; and Elizabeth, who lived to the age of seven.

Young James (later to become president) was nine in 1760 when the family moved to the new brick house, to be known as Montpelier. Nelly spent the rest of her life there. It was a life she apparently enjoyed, and in her later years, she lived quite independently from James and Dolley, with her own rooms, servants and kitchen arrangements. The rooms she used were left unchanged through the years of the duPont ownership of Montpelier. The wainscoting was a light color, probably some shade of white originally, with small closets cut into it and a doorway to stairs leading down to the kitchen.

Nelly was noted as being rather sickly as a young woman and did not expect to have a long life. There is no way to know the nature of her ailments, except from a request from her husband that James get for her use fourteen ounces of quinine, a common treatment for malaria, on one of his trips to Williamsburg.

What further we know of Nelly is left in descriptions of people who visited Montpelier after James's term as president had ended and he and Dolley had returned to Orange County. Among them is the best description of her life at that point, written by Dolley's niece, Mary Cutts:

Mrs. Madison Senior, or "the old Lady" as she was usually called kept up the primitive hours for meals to which she had been accustomed, and her time for receiving visits from the guests of her son was after her dinner and before his.

Mr. Madison honored and loved his mother; his house was the resort of the distinguished men of the time…they esteemed it a privilege to be taken at two o'clock, her audience hour, from the pictured hall and mirror walls, to the old time wainscoted and closeted rooms of this most excellent woman! She was proud of her son who had never given her a moment's anxiety, save for his health, during a long life.

She was a lady of excellent education, strong mind and good judgment, active and well to her last moments; she took an interest in present, modern events as well as the many friends by whom she was surrounded; the love and admiration she bestowed on her daughter in law, who studied her comfort, was ever apparent. She lived to be ninety eight, her usual seat was on a couch in the center of a large room, a table in front, on which was her Bible, prayer book and knitting; these divided her time. The gloves and stockings, with the name knit in were precious gifts to her grandchildren. Our earliest recollection is of seeing Madam de Neuville (wife of the French Minister) sitting near the old Lady talking of the French Revolution and darning a Camel's hair shawl, in which we could see no beauty—but which, she said, was very handsome.

James K. Paulding, a member of Madison's Naval Board, left these impressions of Mother Madison when he visited the family in 1818: "The old Lady seldom joined the family circle but took her meals by herself, and was visited every day by Mr. and Mrs. Madison whom I used often to accompany. She was quite cheerful, in full possession of her faculties, and lived some years after my visit."

Margaret Bayard Smith, the wife of Samuel Harrison Smith, editor of Washington's *National Intelligencer*, described Nelly in a short biography of Dolley, written for a collection of paintings at the National Portrait Gallery. She wrote:

It was considered a great favor and distinction by the gay visitors who thronged Mr. Madison's hospitable mansion, to be admitted to pay the homage of their respects to his reverend mother. The last time the writer of this article enjoyed that privilege, she was then in her ninety-seventh year. She still retained all her faculties, through not free from the bodily infirmities of age. She was sitting, or rather reclining on a couch, beside her was a small table filled with large, dark and worn quartos and folios, of most venerable appearance. She closed one as we entered, and took up her knitting which lay beside her. Among other inquiries, I asked her how she passed her time. "I am never at a loss," she replied; "this and these," touching her knitting and her books, "keep me always busy."

The Baron de Montlezun visited the Madisons in 1816 and met "the old lady" at that time:

Mrs. Madison, mother of the President, came down to meet them. She is eighty-six years old and enjoys perfect health; her memory is good; she is still a very active woman and busies herself with the different occupations of her sex, as in the flower of her youth. Mrs. Madison was born in Virginia; she was delicate and a semi-invalid until her seventieth year. At that age, ordinarily the term of life, her health improved. She had twelve children, of whom only two are still living. I chatted with her about the War of Independence and General Cornwallis. He instilled a great deal of terror, she told me.

Dolley Madison and her mother-in-law had a loving relationship, and Nelly was one of those who helped care for Dolley when she suffered from inflammatory arthritis in 1804.

Margaret Bayard Smith paid a second visit to Montpelier in 1828 and recorded a tender moment between the two Mrs. Madisons:

In the course of the evening, at my request Mrs. M. took me to see old Mrs. Madison. She lacks but 3 years of being a hundred years old. When I enquired of her how she was, "I have been a blest woman," she replied, "blest all my life, and blest in my old age. I have no sickness, no pain excepting my hearing, my senses are but little impaired. I pass my time in reading and knitting." Something being said of the infirmities of old age. "You" she said looking at Mrs. M., "are my mother now, and take care of me in my old age."

When Nelly died, she was buried in the Montpelier cemetery, located near the site of the original Mount Pleasant house. Her grave is next to her husband, James Sr., and to the left of the obelisk marking James's burial place. In addition to his grave, that of Dolley's and those of seven of his brothers and sisters also are located there.

Excavations in 1999 and 2000 at the cemetery, which contains mostly unmarked burial sites, occurred near the 250th anniversary of President James Madison's birth. The oldest grave is that of Ambrose Madison, and the latest is that of Susan Daniel Madison, who died in 1938, the third great-granddaughter of Ambrose and Frances. The brick walls enclose the remains of members of a remarkable American family.

The author thanks Tom Chapman, research coordinator at the Montpelier Foundation, for assistance. The website address for his thesis, "Who Was Buried in James Madison's Grave?" is found at http://www.montpelier.org/library/index.php#archaeology.

Montpelier's Garden

Gardens are a lot like people. They grow and are influenced by their surroundings, their climate, their opportunities and those who love them.

Old gardens can reveal the tastes, times, traditions and needs of the various owners who have cared for them. The garden at Montpelier is a good example.

What lies within the two-acre walled space at the Madison family home was probably begun as a garden in about 1760 when James Madison Sr., father of the future president of the United States, moved his family from their original modest home nearby to the finer structure, with its commanding viewpoint, now restored to its original appearance.

By the time the Montpelier property was inherited by James Madison Jr. in 1801, the garden encompassed four acres. Madison engaged the services of a French gardener, Bizet, whose name evolved into the local patois and spelling of "Beezee." He and his wife had come to Virginia soon after the French Revolution and returned to France in 1836, shortly before Madison died. He was paid $700 per year, a goodly sum at the time, and trained some of the Madison slaves as assistant gardeners.

Like other plantation owners, Madison and his friend Thomas Jefferson often both conferred and competed. Each kept records of wind

View of the Montpelier garden.

and weather, daily fluctuations in temperature and plant growth that would have been valuable aids to Bizet.

Typical of the time, the garden was both practical and ornamental, as chronicled by Mary Cutts, Dolley Madison's niece:

> *The choicest fruits, especially pears, were raised in abundance, figs bore their two crops every summer, which Mr. Madison liked to gather himself, arbors of grapes, over which he exercised the same authority. It was a paradise of roses and other flowers, to say nothing of the strawberries, and vegetables, every rare plant was sent to him by his admiring friends, who knew his tastes, and they were carefully studied and reared by the gardener and his black aids.*

The huge black walnut and cedar of Lebanon trees just outside the present garden wall were probably planted at this time. Tulips, peonies, daffodils, primroses, snowdrops and blue and white hyacinths expressed the glories of spring. Herbs were used in the kitchen and for medicinal purposes.

Even while living in Washington, while serving as secretary of state for Jefferson and during his own presidency following, Madison and his wife, Dolley, kept Montpelier as the family home, where his mother also resided. They enlarged the house, refined the grounds, constructed a garden temple over an icehouse and screened outbuildings with trees. They established broad lawns, natural woodland borders and open vistas, with clumps of large native trees throughout the lawn. The changes gave the property the look of a English estate of the period.

Madison died in 1836. Eight years later, the impoverished Dolley was compelled to sell Montpelier and move to Washington, where she spent her remaining five years. A half dozen owners of the property spanned the following fifty-seven years, using the garden primarily for growing vegetables.

William duPont Sr. purchased Montpelier in 1901, and it became the permanent home of the family: himself, his wife (the former Anna Rodgers) and their two children, Marion and William Jr., then ages eight and six, respectively.

The family had been living in England and, like many wealthy people in the prosperous years between 1880 and the 1930s, traveled widely and were great admirers of the architecture and gardens of Europe. The English landscape tradition loved by the duPonts was alive and well on Montpelier's broad reaches.

Dead, diseased and overly mature native trees were replaced with exotic specimens; ornamental shrubs and perennial beds were replanted, along with boxwood hedges; and a circular driveway was constructed. By 1909, the old landscape had begun a new life.

Twenty years after her arrival at Montpelier, Anna duPont described the garden as they had found it:

> *This was Montpelier's vegetable garden. It had a Virginia worm fence across the bottom of the garden, a paling fence on the other three sides, and a paling gate. The only path was the earth incline path from the entrance to the foot of the garden. The box hedge was broken, bare at the bottom and overgrown on top when we got it. Small terraces had been plowed down, no walk, no path, no tile edging, no grass, no vases, no flowers—just a wilderness of weeds. It has taken twenty-two years to get the box in its present shape. All the planting of trees and shrubs and flowers were my designs.*

Montpelier garden gate.

The garden continued to develop in a formal manner, possibly influenced by the ideas of the prominent English plantswoman Gertrude Jeykle, whose books were in the library. Gravel paths were edged with glazed tiles from Georgia. Lions, urns, a sundial and Italian columns were imported from Europe. A brick wall was built to keep the cattle out, and lacy wrought-iron gates were hung.

Definition and structure were provided by box and privet hedges, while roses flourished in beds and on trellises. Terraces were crisscrossed with grass walks and set off by topiary. Flowers, shrubs, fruit and ornamental trees graced the broad spans of this garden, providing drama and color from spring through fall.

Marion duPont Scott inherited Montpelier in 1928 and kept it as her primary residence throughout her lifetime. Horses were Marion's lifelong passion, as evidenced by the steeplechase races she began that continue to be held there every autumn, but she still maintained an interest in the garden.

Its redesign was delegated to noted Richmond landscape architect Charles F. Gillette, whose fame was based on his skill in adapting traditional forms and styles to the Virginia landscape. Under his hand, elaborate brickwork replaced the grass paths in the formal rose garden, new evergreens and shrubs were added and parterres were created on the lower lawn.

Marion died in 1983, and in 1984, her wish for guardianship of Montpelier by the National Trust for Historic Preservation was realized. The garden, by that time, needed another major effort.

Funded by the Garden Club of Virginia, the two-year restoration began in October 1990. The overgrown boxwood hedges again were brought under control, an irrigation system was put in, brickwork was repointed and stone steps were installed. Steel edgings contained the flower beds, which held more than eighty varieties of daylilies, iris, narcissus and peonies. These were dug and transplanted into the old cutting garden, while the soil in their beds was amended. Careful records of the colors, fragrance and blooming times were maintained. By 1991, the crescent and border beds were redesigned using this original plant material.

Echoes of the garden's 1760s origins are found in the herb beds in the front parterres and in the roses that still climb the brick wall along the "lover's lane." A new fence was built near the bottom of the garden, replacing the one Marion had there. Visitors love to wander the paths, inspect the plant varieties and observe the view.

"The most frequently heard comments from visitors to the garden is how peaceful and calming it is," says Montpelier's horticulturist, Sandy Mudrinich. "I attribute this to its layout and design, which includes a perfect blend of useful flowers beds interspersed with the restful spans of green lawn."

The Montpelier Train Station

The small, charming building on Route 20 South known locally as the Montpelier Train Station has provided important community functions in its lifetime. In its present life, it continues to do so, serving as the local Montpelier Station Post Office, as well as housing an exhibit of African American history from the Jim Crow era.

Early in the twentieth century, the Southern Railroad Company, for which William duPont was a board member, bought a right of way through his Montpelier property to connect the town of Orange with Charlottesville. The passage was granted providing that the railroad make plans available for a depot, with scheduled passenger and freight stops at Montpelier as well.

The station was constructed from local lumber by Montpelier employees in 1910; it served as a passenger station from 1912 to 1929 and for freight from 1911 to 1962. Built with a hip roof with dormers and a six-foot overhang, its original plans are located in Special Collections at the University of Virginia Library.

A centrally located window backed by horizontal iron bars on the highway side of the building boasts the post office logo of an eagle. A door was there originally that led into the post office on the right, or west, side of the building. The waiting rooms for train passengers were located on the east end, roughly divided with two-thirds of the space for use by white people on the tracks side. A sign designated the other one-third for "Colored," and mailboxes were built into the west wall of that room, which was also the post office lobby. The four original benches, two for each room, are back in place, and post office functions continue in the west end of the structure.

In addition, the structure was the home of the stationmasters, who probably also served as postmasters, as well as a great many termites. The termites have been eradicated, and master carpenter Mark Gooch dealt with the damage they left by reinforcing floor joists and replacing wall studs. Otherwise the building materials are in extremely fine condition.

Two stationmasters left their marks with notations on the walls. One reads: "Ed Young, stationmaster 1928–1951," and the other, "I.P. Hall, July 2, 1950 to 1954." The stationmasters were also telegraphers and worked near where a Western Union logo remains on the wall. Gooch found many narrow rolls of paper that had been tossed up into the roof overhang that were covered with handwritten messages sent

Montpelier Station interior.

over the telegraph wires, which still remain in the wall. One that had been sent to a veterinarian in Staunton noted, "Mare still down. Bring sling," signed by William duPont. The messages now are part of the Montpelier archives.

The stationmasters had living quarters on the second floor, accessed by a small doorway on the highway side of the building. The space, occupied until 1950, consists of four rooms, some with beautiful windows of little three- by five-inch diamond-shaped panes, a number of which Gooch has carefully replaced. In order to have the new panes undecipherable from the original ones, he was able to recut old glass that came either from windows removed from the duPont additions to the mansion or from local people who stopped by to offer similar material.

"People have been wonderful." said Director of Restoration John Jeanes. "They have come by to offer old materials and stories, both at the mansion and here at the station. This oral history is invaluable, and we are archiving it. We hope people will continue to add to this very important collection."

There never was running water or indoor plumbing in the building, but there is a standpipe outside. This was changed when the renovation was completed, and the upstairs area has become office space for Montpelier staff. Pipes and fixtures for gaslights in the building remain in place, however, as do the knob and tube wiring and switches, along with the hand-cranked telephone.

The basement freight loading room measures about eleven by twenty-one feet and has an early-model Otis elevator that is still useful. Mail and freight from train cars came directly into the basement and then were lifted to the ground floor when needed. A heavy rolling door on the highway side allowed bulky freight items to be collected. That door, with its original hardware, remains, locked in place but still operable. A smaller door has been installed with two sidelights, leading into the post office side of the building.

An exhibit of African American history has been installed in the space that had been designated as the "Colored" waiting room. It draws the curve from the era of slavery on the Montpelier plantation through the transition to emancipation with the Gilmore cabin and finally personifies

The Montpelier Train Station served passengers and freight shipments, as well as postal patrons.

the Jim Crow era. "The African American Historical Society," says its spokesman, Mat Reeves, "has worked with Montpelier to make the restoration of the train station applicable to the local community and to Orange County in general."

Somehow, an intense sense of reality permeates the beautiful little station. This is where all of the factions of the community centered. They met one another here to pass the news, enjoy conversation, perhaps flirt and, yes, even gossip. They took train trips of a lifetime. They saw family members off and met them upon their return. They sent and received important messages by telegraph. They collected their mail, picked up new farm machinery and marveled at shipments from Sears Roebuck and Montgomery Ward that would be assembled into huge barns on the Montpelier property. Sadly, even coffins from World War I arrived at the station.

Burly diesel-powered trains charge on by without stopping now, but with a little imagination the asthmatic whistles of the old steam engines still echo in the small station.

George Gilmore, Freed Madison Slave

A modest log cabin sitting a few hundred feet from Route 20 near the entrance to Montpelier catches the eye and the imagination. It re-creates significant eras of local history, first in the persona of a freed slave who had been able to buy his home from the Madison family at age ninety after thirty years of rent and mortgage payments, and second as a site of a huge Civil War encampment.

The story of the George Gilmore family took some digging, literally and figuratively. Information gathered from Orange County property and census records, as well as those of the Freedmen's Bureau, combined with archaeological findings and oral history to put together the story of the family who lived there.

These sources indicate that George Gilmore was born either in 1810 or 1813, the son of another George Gilmore, a carpenter, who was one of the ninety-seven slaves owned by President James Madison.

The younger George worked as a carpenter at Montpelier as well and also learned saddle making. He was listed in official Freedmen's Bureau records in 1867 as being one of only six "colored men" in Orange County who could read and write and also that he was "of good character." County census records listed him as a mulatto. His wife, Polly, who may also have worked at Montpelier, is remembered by a family member as being a full-blooded Cherokee.

Gilmore cabin, Montpelier.

The couple had eight children between the years of 1859 and 1867. The five who survived to adulthood were Philip, Jeremiah, William, Mildred and Ida.

In 1870, five years after the Emancipation Proclamation, the family was living in the area where their two-story cabin now stands. It was built by 1873 on property leased from Dr. James Madison and was located near his residence.

George was working as a farmhand and saddle maker, as well as whatever else someone hired him to do. Census records show that by 1880 he had risen from the status of farm laborer to that of farmer, a point reached by only 11 percent of African Americans at that time. He had cleared and planted twelve of his sixteen acres and owned a horse, two cows, four pigs and eleven poultry. For tax purposes, his property was evaluated at twenty-six dollars.

Polly was listed in the census as "keeping house." Being at home was a matter of pride, and it indicated that she did not have to work for other people but instead attended to the many tasks of running a household and raising children. Seven thousand beads, as well as many needles and pins found in the cabin fireboxes, show that Polly and probably at least one of the girls were also engaged in sewing, since the beads were of the type used in fashionable shawls of the period.

By 1900, William, the youngest son, then age thirty-five, and his wife, Bertha, twenty-one, also shared the home. Their two children, Ollie and Onie, increased the family to three generations.

The 1900 census also shows that by that year George held a mortgage for the property. On February 28, 1901, shortly before Dr. Madison's death, they received the deed that indicates that George, then ninety years old, had purchased 16.1 acres for $560 after those thirty years of rent and mortgage payments. George lived there four more years until his death, and Polly died three years later in 1908. The children buried them in the family plot on what had truly become, finally, their own land.

Unfortunately, George had died intestate. Various needs of his children brought an effort to have the property divided, and it was decided by the county judge that since it was "not susceptible of division," it would be auctioned and the proceeds shared by four of George's descendants.

The best bid at the auction, said to be unusually high, was $4,687. It added the Gilmore's farm to the adjacent property of William duPont, who had purchased Montpelier in 1900.

Part of the family continued to live in the home until, unable to keep it up sufficiently, three moved to Somerset. The others left Virginia to migrate north.

After that, improvements such as a stove, wallboard and linoleum were put in, and it was used by duPont employees until it became vacant in the 1970s. As part of the Montpelier property, it was deeded to the National Trust for Historic Preservation in Marion duPont Scott's will in 1984.

Queries from the Gilmore family regarding the cabin and family cemetery, both in very poor condition, resulted in research from the Montpelier restoration team and consultants from the Colonial Williamsburg Foundation to bring eventual restoration to the cabin in 2004.

By the summer of 2005, the trowels of a team of students from the State University of New York were producing their iconic *scritch-scratch* (music to an archaeologist) that indicated that serious research was in

Gilmore archaeology, Montpelier.

progress. The field of action was behind the cabin, where Montpelier's director of archaeology, Matthew Reeves, says that they found the rock base of one of the cabins built during the Civil War, probably for use by a Confederate officer.

During the winter of 1863–64, before the Battle of the Wilderness, the Montpelier property had been occupied by nine Confederate regiments from North and South Carolina under command of Generals McGowan and Wilcox. The area where the cabin now stands, on the north side of Route 20, had been cleared and laid out in militarily precise rows with huts built by and for the troops.

The huts generally would be made of logs, with a piece of canvas tossed over the top for a roof. Orange County records show that some of these abandoned structures, especially those of a better quality used by officers, were sometimes occupied by local people after the armies moved on.

Reeves said that the Gilmores used salvaged materials from the abandoned huts to build their first home, just twelve feet square in size.

Detail of Gilmore cabin structure.

By 1873, the family had begun building a one-and-a-half-story log cabin in their "front yard" using stones from the chimney of the earlier home, which was then being used as a workshop or shed, as seen in a 1910 photo. The National Trust for Historic Preservation became the owner of the Montpelier property, including the Gilmore cabin, in 1984. Restoration of the cabin, which was on the verge of collapse at that point, began in 2000 when Rebecca Gilmore Coleman, Orange County native and great-granddaughter of George Gilmore, brought the structure to the attention of the Montpelier Foundation, to which she donated a portion of the original farm. She also gave her time and energy, as well as information about her family that permitted the entire farm to be preserved and interpreted.

Remembering Life
at Rockwood

Mildred Benton Brookings spent more than seventy-five years at Rockwood, located on Chicken Mountain Road. Here life centered on the annual steeplechase races at Montpelier, the fall hunting season and the pack of foxhounds that her husband, Linwood "Link" Brooking, managed for Marion duPont Scott.

Mildred grew up at Locust Hill in Madison County, where she and Link met on the back porch on a blind date. "He had a car with a rumble seat," she recalled. "He was courting another girl, but I guess he liked me because he asked me for a second date."

They were married in 1934 and lived with his parents for six months until they moved to Rockwood, a property that Marion duPont Scott had purchased in 1929 to expand her hunting area. She had the house fixed up for the Brookings to live in and conveyed it to them in 1961. Their children, Ann Brooking Stelter and her brother, Curtis, were born in the main-floor bedroom.

Their father, Link, also was born at home, on Five Oaks Farm in the Montford area, and had been working with Scott's horses since 1929, the year the Montpelier racetrack was built. He became huntsman, the person in charge of the foxhounds for the hunts, in 1934. That was the first year of the Montpelier Hunt Race Meet, for which he acted as patrol judge, leading the horses to the starting post decked

The Rockwood House.

Ann Brooking Stelter on the Rockwood House porch.

out in a traditional pink coat, for which he had been measured by Scott's tailor in New York.

"In addition to being Link's boss," says Mildred, "Mrs. Scott also was a friend. She liked to come here. She followed and entered horses in the big races—the Derby, the Preakness and Belmont."

The fox hunting circuit was a big time, usually with a field of eighteen to twenty riders that included Scott's good friends. The hounds were kept further up the mountain and were brought to summer kennels at Rockwood in 1935. Rockwood became the year-round kennel location in the 1940s, and the structures are still there, used now for storage.

"The horses and riders convened at Rockwood," continued Mildred. "The hounds were released, and the hunt began. Sometimes they would strike a fox—or not—right on the place. At first there weren't many deer, but the number grew to be very prevalent. Of course, the hounds were hard to control and would chase the deer. As a result, they began to hunt in Madison County quite a lot, where there were not so many deer."

"The hounds were fed by Major Smith," added Ann. "That was his name, not a military rank. He cooked them up great pans of cornbread in the kennel kitchen."

The kennel at Rockwood was the breeding center for the pack, the American foxhound. They were registered and sometimes were sold or traded. Scott's love of dogs extended to whippets, which she also showed. A pair of the breed sculpted by Carroll Bassett was moved from the back portico of the mansion at Montpelier to the Bassett House—Carroll's home that became the residence of the president of the Montpelier Foundation, Michael Quinn, and his wife, Carolyn.

Scott also had border terriers and gave a renowned birthday party for one, Wallace. The first sanctioned border terrier match was held at Montpelier in 1957.

Ann cherished her memories of growing up with her brother at Rockwood: "We used to love to see the puppies and play with them. My dad let us do that, but I don't think he really liked it much. These were working animals, they weren't pets, and both they and we knew their place. I used to look at the kennel and think, 'Those foxhounds really have it good. They have a front porch where they can sit and

Mrs. Brooking in Rockwood House parlor.

look out and even a swimming pool (dip tank),' and I didn't have a swimming pool!"

Ann and Curtis went through the Orange County school system, from which she graduated in 1952. Mildred drove them into town, and during the war, to save gas, she stayed in town with Link's mother until time to pick up the children. Ann remembered that the ladies spent time doing various things to support the war effort, such as making bandages out of old bedsheets.

"Thanksgiving Day was the event of the year at our house," recalled Ann. "Not because of the 'thankful feast,' but because it was hog killing time. My dad raised hogs, and they butchered them and put most of the meat into the meat house, where it was cured by salting and smoking.

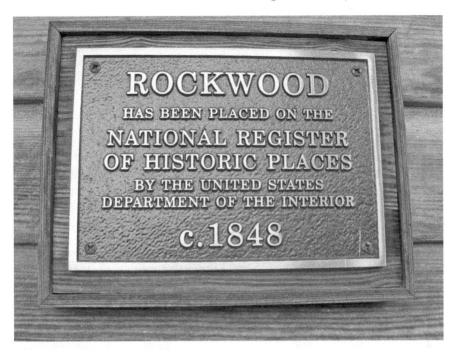

Rockwood House historical plaque.

The fat was put into a large pot over an outdoor fire and 'rendered,' or boiled, to melt to make lard. My dad had us toss in potatoes that whitened the lard, and we ate them and thought they were the best things we ever tasted!" The meat house later became the kennel for the Norwich terriers.

Ann graduated from Longwood College with degrees in sociology and English and then spent two years as a social worker in Fairfax and Winchester Counties before attending graduate school at Tulane. She and Ted, who had met in Fairfax, married in 1961 and went to Florida, where they raised three sons, with frequent visits to Orange. They split their time between West Palm Beach and a log cabin that they built on two acres at Five Oaks Farm, part of land that has belonged to the Brookings family since before the Civil War, and where her loyalties lie.

Always proud of her ancestry, Ann's favorite line is, "To be a Virginian, either by immigration or adoption, or even one's mother's side, is an introduction to any state in the Union, a passport to any foreign country and a benediction from above."

Gordon's Inn

The Beginning of a Town

The town of Gordonsville began on property that had been acquired in 1728 by Ambrose Madison, grandfather of future U.S. president James Madison. Fifty-nine years later, in 1787, the owner was the president's cousin, Thomas Madison, who sold 1,350 acres of the original plantation to Nathaniel Gordon, who named it Newville.

In Virginia's agrarian society, the wealth lay in the land. Although the acreage that Gordon bought no doubt had value for farming, his future financial success and fame lay not in agriculture but in a commercial venture to establish a business, the Gordon Inn, to accommodate travelers.

The location was perfect. Two well-used roads intersected on the property, the Fredericksburg Great Road that came from the northeast and another that led west between Richmond and the Valley of Virginia. Gordon was the first postmaster in the area by 1813, and the town that grew up around him became known as Gordonsville.

Taverns had served important functions since early colonial times, when by law there had to be an establishment every twenty miles on the few existing roads. These would serve as places for people to rest, eat, drink, socialize, exchange news, no doubt to gamble a little, perhaps acquire a fresh horse and leave or collect messages. It is no surprise that they often became designated as official post offices.

The terms "tavern" and "inn" were interchangeable, and generally speaking, they were male strongholds, since women in that period did not travel often and rarely, if ever, traveled alone. Even if accompanied by a husband, they probably would take overnight accommodations in a private home that offered hospitality similar to our modern B&Bs, since even the best taverns were known to become rowdy at times and certainly offered very little privacy.

Evidence that Gordon's inn could accommodate at least a dozen people is shown in the probate inventory of his possessions when he died in 1820. They included "two high bedsteads, ten common bedsteads, and 12 feather beds."

A high bedstead would indicate that there was room enough under it to store another bed, which was pulled out when needed. These were known as trundle beds, the word "trundle" being an early term meaning "to drag." That many featherbeds would mean that the patrons were provided more luxury than a mattress stuffed with straw, which was expected to be found in lesser establishments.

The Gordon Inn had a reputation as "a good house," and Thomas Jefferson, who spoke from personal experience as a patron there, recommended it as such to Georgia governor John Milledge in 1802. Some other well-known Virginians who stayed there were James Monroe, Henry Clay, Phillip and James Barbour and John Randolph of Roanoke. It also hosted the Marquis de Lafayette in 1824, two years after the death of Nathaniel Gordon.

Such dignitaries as those mentioned surely would have been offered a private room, but men of lesser prestige would not have been surprised, indeed usually would have expected, to find more than one bed in a room. If the tavern was crowded, they could rent not a room but rather a space in a bed that would be shared with another person, not necessarily someone with whom he was acquainted. This custom was particularly common in towns that had courthouses when, during court sessions and especially during political elections, crowded taverns gave dimension to the old expression that politics makes strange bedfellows.

The Gordon Inn ceased to be operated as such by 1830. It was the private home of Mrs. Mary Barbour when Stonewall Jackson stayed there recuperating for three weeks during the Civil War. It was torn down in 1940 after further use as a school building.

The town was reaching its growth potential by 1840, and prosperity was aided by the development of rail transport. It was the year that the Louisa Railroad (which became known as the Virginia Central in 1850 and then the Chesapeake and Ohio in 1868 and now is CSX) connected the town east to Richmond and west to the Valley of Virginia. By 1860, the Orange and Alexandria Railroad was bringing passengers and freight from the North.

Although transportation by rail obviously was easier and more comfortable than traveling by foot, horseback or stagecoach, it would cause many complaints today. Rail passengers could, for instance, expect to spend eight hours traveling between Alexandria and Gordonsville, making many stops and conforming to various regulations, including a speed limit of four miles per hour over bridges. Passengers also contended with delays due to weather, accidents or obstructions on the track, such as roving animals.

Schedules improved over time, but passengers coming into Gordonsville on one line and expecting to transfer to the other might have a considerable wait, perhaps overnight, before making connections. In order to offer these passengers better accommodations than waiting in a depot, Richard Flint Omohundro obtained a license in 1840 to build an establishment adjacent to the Louisa Railroad depot called an eating house. This name obviously indicates that it served meals and possibly was designed to accommodate families, but there is no substantiating evidence that this was the case.

The building burned down in 1859, and Omohundro immediately contracted with master builder Benjamin Faulconer to construct another on the site. When Henry Jones bought the property in 1862, it included a tavern house, a stable, a corn house, a kitchen and other outbuildings necessary to run such an enterprise. Somewhere in this time period, it began to be known as the Exchange Hotel since it was the point where passengers could have comfortable conditions when changing from one rail line to another.

The local *Gordonsville Gazette* newspaper issue of November 22, 1859, characterized Omohundro's business acumen at that point by noting that he "made the beginning of a large fortune. He was particularly adapted to this vocation; being of a genial, social disposition and regarding with great concert the comfort of his numerous guests with a liberal hand, it was not surprising that his popularity as a landlord was universal."

Then came April 12, 1861, with the attack on Fort Sumter in Charleston, South Carolina, and the ensuing war that brought a new role to the Exchange Hotel and impact to the town of Gordonsville.

The Exchange Hotel

Gordonsville's Receiving Hospital, 1861–1865

When the Civil War began, the rails that had brought commerce and travel from four directions into Gordonsville were given a new role. Railroads became an important factor in the conflict, since they could quickly transport supplies and reinforcements, improve communications and carry sick and wounded soldiers away from the battlefields.

All of these elements flowed through Gordonsville, where in November 1862 a Union scout reported "large army supplies" being stored in the depot and other buildings, awaiting trans-shipment.

Although the scout's report did not mention it, a major Confederate military hospital had been established there in August 1861. It existed in the building owned by Henry Jones that had been constructed a year or two earlier by Richard Flint Omohundro, a railroad contractor, for use as a hotel.

Basically, there were two types of military hospitals that functioned during this period: receiving and forwarding hospitals and general hospitals.

Located along rail lines, receiving and forwarding hospitals gave further treatment to patients who had received first aid on the battleground. Unless their condition was too serious to travel farther, they stayed for only a day or two before being sent forward to general hospitals

The Exchange Hotel, Gordonsville.

that had capacity and supplies to give treatments for an indefinite time. Gordonsville's Exchange Hotel became one of the major thirty-nine receiving and forwarding hospitals along the Virginia rail lines, sending patients onward to Charlottesville, Richmond, Hanover, Lynchburg and Staunton for further care.

Conflicts through August 1862 brought wounded from both armies to Gordonsville, all of whom received equal care. The Moore Hospital at Manassas had been discontinued that month, and its wooden pavilion tents, with a bed capacity of about one thousand men, were reassembled in Gordonsville. The space surrounding the hospital became covered with tents and other shelters that are said to have numbered as many as two hundred.

It is a generally held fact that more soldiers died from diseases than from battle wounds. Of about 600,000 Confederate soldiers, nearly 200,000 died. Of these, about 50,000 deaths resulted from wounds, leaving about 150,000 who died from diseases. The most common diseases were typhoid, smallpox and measles. Records show that more of the patients at the Gordonsville hospital were treated for diarrhea and pneumonia than for battle wounds.

A pest house for smallpox patients was established one mile away from the hospital, across the Orange County line into Louisa County, and a quarantine camp for those with measles was nearby. The surgeon in charge of the pest house was Dr. Edward A. Craighill. In his memoirs, published in 1905, he described the pest house as "a shanty, which eventually grew to be quite a house in a retired place in the woods, for the treatment of small pox patients exclusively." Dr. Craighill visited it every morning and at other times when needed. He said that he vaccinated himself daily and kept his "small pox clothes in the woods in the open air when not in service."

The hospital complex, however, was an entity almost entirely unto itself. In addition to the pavilion tents from Manassas, it consisted of a "dead house" or mortuary, as well as the buildings originally surrounding the hotel, "a Tavern House, Stable, Corn House, Kitchen, an eating house, a bakery, and an ice house."

It is known that other buildings in the town were forced, at times, into use as medical facilities of one type or another. They included private homes, the basement of the Baptist church, the freight depot, the Moyers and Jones Chair Factory and the Gordonsville Chair and Agricultural Implement Factory.

Dr. B.M. Lebby, originally from South Carolina, was surgeon in charge at the hospital for more than three years. About 5,000 to 6,000 men were treated in Gordonsville during the war, as many as 2,000 in a single one-week period. In spite of those huge numbers, death rosters carry the names of only 740 men.

Staffing was a monumental problem, and Dr. Lebby depended heavily on local residents to supply the hospital's needs. Employed at the facility were five medical officers, a chaplain, two clerks, two stewards, one or two ward masters, a head matron, about four matrons, about thirty (male) nurses, five to ten laundresses and a few cooks and bakers. They received the equivalent of an enlisted man's pay, $18.50 per month.

African American men, both slave and free, were highly sought as nurses by the military hospitals, since nursing, which required personal care and tending of patients, was not considered to be a respectable occupation for women, especially white women. Dr. Lebby complained at one time that he was having a hard time finding people.

In spite of the many difficult problems he faced, Dr. Lebby was doing a good job. In a letter to his brother, dated January 6, 1865, he wrote, "I can assure you that I have been complimented very high both by the Surgeon General and the Inspector as having one of the best and neatest hospitals in the State."

He continued: "Do come and see the Town of Gordonsville which the Yankees so often tried to capture but failed in every attempt. They very nearly captured it on the week before Christmas they having got one and a half miles from Town, about 5,000 strong but fortunately for Gordonsville, Genl. Lee sent two S.C. Brigades up here and they arrived about one hour before the devils got so near and as soon as they heard the whistle of the Engine, they turned tail and ran like a flock of sheep."

The hospital was closed in June 1865, and the federal government turned the main building into a branch of the Bureau of Refugees, Freedmen and Abandoned Lands. Established by Congress that year and known familiarly as the Freedmen's Bureau, its mission was to aid former black troops and emancipated people by attempting to safeguard their rights, ensure fair treatment, provide social services and adjudicate legal cases. These responsibilities were transferred to individual states four years later, and the bureau was discontinued except for educational efforts that resulted in establishing nearly three thousand schools and the founding of black colleges and normal schools.

Richard Flint Omohundro, who had constructed the building originally, sued for the right to repossess the property. The case was lost in federal court, and it was sold at auction to Mr. J.W. Christmas, who operated it as a hotel, as did the last business owner of record, John B. Parrott, who ran it from 1922 to 1937.

After that, it sat empty, except for the vagrants and vandals who did major damage to the interior. The chimneys, long left uncleaned and unrepaired, were not usable, so fires were lit on floors in three downstairs rooms, and the staircase served as fuel. Eventually, even the vagrants left it to a heavy growth of vines, trees and shrubbery that reached to the second floor and blocked the doorways and broken windows.

This was unacceptable to one longtime Gordonsville resident, Mrs. Gladys Cowherd, who owned a small business in town. She rallied friends, businessmen and the local historical society to help save the building, and she and her female friends worked diligently, even laying the new floors themselves. It was opened in 1988 as the Exchange Hotel, owned by Historic Gordonsville, Inc.

A widely anticipated living history event has taken place annually since 1993, variously hosting units from the Thirty-third Virginia Infantry, part of Stonewall's Brigade, and the Seventh Virginia Cavalry from Culpeper. Also involved have been doctors affiliated with the National Civil War Medical Museum of Frederick, Maryland, as well as interpretations held of the activities of black Confederate soldiers and telegraphers. Food is prepared by descendants of the famed "chicken ladies," who, since the earliest days, served meals to passengers through train windows until the appearance of dining cars and air conditioning sealed the open windows and ended their business.

Christ Church Reflects
Its English Roots

In the year 1875, Ulysses S. Grant was president, Albert Schweitzer was born, Mark Twain published *Tom Sawyer*, Stanley met Livingston and an early form of the typewriter was invented. In addition, on October 10 of that year in Gordonsville, the first service was held at Christ Episcopal Church.

Although that event was to have no national or international impact, to the local parishioners it certainly was a memorable day. It had required a true test of Episcopal grit, determination and faith to have to travel a total of up to twenty-five miles or more, either on top of or behind a horse, to attend services at Saint Thomas in Orange or to the chapel in Somerset. One man had succeeded in alleviating that situation.

He was Bolling Walker Haxall, resident of Richmond, president of Old Dominion Iron and Steel Works and partner in Haxall's Mill. In 1862, Haxall had purchased a property near Gordonsville known as Springfield from the heirs of Colonel Rueben Lindsay, a Revolutionary War officer who had settled there. In addition to his involvement in farming at Springfield, Haxall had also developed an interest in the local community.

Haxall met with other Episcopalians, and they formed a splinter group under the canonical control of Saint Thomas Parish. The first services were held in a hexagonal stone tower at Springfield. With perhaps twenty-nine or so communicants, the congregation had increased sufficiently by September 1874 to require a priest in residence, and the members engaged Reverend Frank Garrett Scott to lead them. In May a year later, they achieved all of the rights, privileges and responsibilities of a separate congregation and named it Christ Church, Gordonsville.

Wasting no time, they began in the same month to break ground and begin construction of the building. The total cost of $5,500 for the lot, the building and its contents was financed almost entirely by Haxall. It was not until 1923, however, that the church had developed to the extent that the Diocese of Virginia established it as a separate parish and designated it Scott Parish, honoring the first rector.

Upon catching the first glimpse of Christ Church, it appears, somehow, to have been misdirected by a careless cosmic coachman and dropped into Gordonsville instead of an English country village in Dorset. One can almost hear the sheep bleating on the other side of the brick wall.

The Gothic architecture of the building, with its steeply pitched roof, follows the cruciform of early Anglican churches, with the transept, the arms of the cross, located near the altar. Also, like the early churches, it was aligned east so the congregation faced toward the rising sun, symbol of resurrection. Usually graves were also established the same way.

These are traditions brought by the early English settlers who were not yet Virginians, or even Americans per se, but who had brought with them all of their proud British heritage. Thus, the early parishes in the Virginia colony were Anglican—state churches supported by public funds and performing certain functions, such as caring for the poor and indigent and educating orphans. Likewise, they tended to follow the traditional architecture derived from their homeland.

Rector Alex McPhail, warmly addressed by parishioners as "Father Mac," was quick to explain the architectural design of Christ Church and designate its heritage:

> *They built the church in the Gothic manner to follow the original presence in this country and stay true to the Oxford Movement, beginning around 1823 to 1840, that felt the ritual was becoming anti-ceremonial. They were striving to recover the nature of the roots of the old Catholic Church.*

Likewise, the pews are set in the monastic style, with two sets by the transept positioned to face each other. This is where the monks chanted back and forth to each other, and now they are used by the choir.

The windows in the church were imported from England, and most are painted with a diamond pattern in yellow, white and red. Four are embellished with religious symbols. The windows on either side of the altar have plaques commemorating Francis Robinson Haxall and Charlotte Taylor Haxall Lee, wife of Captain Robert E. Lee Jr. and both relatives of Bolling Haxall; they gave extraordinary support through the years.

Mrs. George Zinn, great-niece of Bolling Haxall, wished to replace the original reed pump organ used since 1876. She donated a diamond ring to be sold as a start for an endowment fund to provide a new instrument, installed in 1931, as a memorial for her son, George Zinn Jr.

Originally, the left wing of the transept at Christ Church was the main entry of the building until 1947, when a narthex was added to the west end of the structure by Flora Cameron Zinn to make a new entrance. This allowed the former entry area to be used for the organ chamber.

In 1970, a fire began in the sacristy, in the right wing of the transept, that affected the area around the altar and caused water damage to the organ. Memorial gifts over the years provided the means to rebuild and enlarge the 1931 instrument, with work done by a parishioner, George Carson of Barboursville, that served well nearly thirty years more.

By 1999, however, a new organ, built in Vienna, Virginia, at more than twice the size of the previous one, had been installed. It has nearly one thousand pipes, replacing the old instrument with fewer than five hundred.

Fortunately, the 1970 fire was contained, so the flames did not seriously affect the rest of the church, but smoke and water damage resulted in redecorating efforts. Wallpaper on canvas backing that simulates stucco with a design of stone blocks was put up, combining nicely with the Gothic-style lamps, the wood hammerbeam roof supports and dark brown planks of the ceiling. The pews were also replaced at that time.

The Parish Hall, built in 1926, reflects the church's architectural style in a simpler manner. It includes space for a parlor, the rector's office, the vestry room, a Sunday school area and a kitchen.

The brick wall and the plantings in the churchyard were projects originally planned and directed by Charles Gillette, a noted landscape architect from Richmond who was known for his expertise in creating natural settings. Again, generous donors contributed toward the project, including Marion duPont Scott, Mrs. Zinn, Alexander Cameron and Mrs. Edwin B. Strange.

Trees specified in the Gillett plans eventually grew to overshadow the church, obscuring it and pushing against the wall with root growth. Necessary adjustments give passing motorists the pleasant visual jolt of the structure's sharply steep and precise angular form, a contrast to the many voluptuous and spreading Victorian buildings in the rest of the town.

The memorial garden in the west end of the yard is the place where "cremains," ashes of those who have been cremated, lie. Other burials, including that of Marion duPont Scott, are at the cemetery on Route 33 West.

The steeple looms over the copper roof, both of which were renewed in the past decade, replacing the original steeple and bell dating from 1877. The bell had not been rung for some time since one of the support beams was broken and its action would dislodge the nests and droppings of the pigeons who had been using it for far too long. Wire barriers inside the new steeple keep the birds away, and the bell again peals loudly and proudly.

Shady Grove School

Y ou love me, yes you do." "I hate Elaine by Adelaide." "I hate Adelaide."

Such passionate personal statements can occur publicly anywhere young children go to school. These are some that happen to be inscribed in pencil on the horizontal boards of the girl's coatroom of Shady Grove School for African American Children, built in 1925 and used until 1954.

The school is located on the grounds of Shady Grove Church that bought it in 1957 and used the small structure variously as a Sunday school building, the church's dining hall and for wedding receptions. Restoration began in 2007 with the help of Ruth and George Long, the church, the Orange County African-American Historical Society and other generous donors.

The graffiti, along with the original chalkboard, the heart pine floors, the student desks and other mementos (including a flag from the period), were all researched and furnished by the Orange High School ROTC students.

Ruth Long researched the class rolls and discovered that there were up to forty-four students per year in attendance. Recurring family names included Alexander, Ellis, Jackson, Lindsay, Long, Poindexter, Richardson, Sawyer, White, Williams and Willis, some of whom are members of the Shady Grove Church. There was no transportation for the students, and her husband, George, who did much of the restoration work at the school, remembered that the Long children had to walk "two miles down the county road and a mile and a half on a road through the woods" to get to school.

The children were under the tutelage of female teachers, two of those being Mrs. Redd and Mrs. Mabel Shirley. The two-room structure measures only nineteen by thirty-four feet, a space that could be separated equally by a two-section door that folded and stacked against the walls. Kerosene lamps that fit into holders mounted on the wall furnished light on dark days. The windows have been repaired, and missing glass has been replaced. George Long said that the slight sagging of the windowsill is from all the times children used it to pull themselves up to see out of the high windows.

Each of the rooms was heated by a stove that shared a single chimney, with two flues repaired by mason Edward Richardson using old bricks found by Albert McGhee Jr. Potbellied stoves have been replaced by one of a different design from the period, and George remembered how the boys were given the task of going out to the coal pile in the yard to replenish the fires.

George sat on a chair in the schoolroom, one knee showing through a winking slit in his work clothes, and he displayed an impish grin as he remembered pranks they played. Some of the most memorable involved the wooden privy that was moved from site to site as usage demanded.

"I reckon there are old filled-up privy holes all over this area," he said, waving his capable, work-stained hand to indicate the back lot. "One thing the big boys did sometimes was tip it over when another boy was in there. You sure came flying out with your britches dragging!" Although George, the eldest of fourteen children, did not admit to being one of the pranksters, his big, ready smile, as well as his energy and outgoing personality, seemed to make that a possibility. He remembered that when he did misbehave, there was no escaping punishment, since the teachers would send a note home with one of his brothers or sisters. Eighty-three-year-old Howard Richardson recalled that misbehavior was punished in class by having the student face the corner standing on one foot. "If the foot came down," he said, "the switch came out."

Shady Grove School is thought to have been in use until the school year of 1953–54, when the new Lightfoot Elementary School in

Unionville was built for African American students and integrated in 1967. Secondary education was offered at the Orange County Colored High School, where students attended in the late 1930s and 1940s. George Washington Carver Regional High School in adjoining Culpeper County served African American students from Orange, Culpeper, Madison and Rappahannock Counties from 1948 to 1968 until full integration took place.

Rebecca Coleman, one of the founders of the Orange County African American Society, said that the Shady Grove School is a prime example of the schools that African American children attended in the mid-twentieth century. The society encouraged Shady Grove Church to restore it and possibly to use it as a museum.

"In our research, we have found over twenty such schools that Orange County provided for its black citizens," she said. "Some of these were mere one-room shacks with no running water, no indoor plumbing or with only a stove to heat the building. There was only one teacher for six grades in one room. We are gathering oral histories from the students and teachers. This research is what our organization is all about. We want America's history to be inclusive. All of its citizens contributed to its history, the good and the bad."

The Peyton Family Personifies
the Village of Rapidan

"We were the workers," she said. "The wealthy people lived on the hill." Ellen Lovell Taylor Donnelly sat in her comfortable home by the Rapidan River and remembered how her family contributed to the community that now has almost disappeared. Its historical and genealogical footprints remain, however, designating the names and lives of the people who made it function.

"There was a whole tribe of us," Ellen continued. "The Peytons, along with the Holladays, Willises and Taliaferros, who were large landowners. Very few are left now, although some are coming back."

The village of Rapidan was originally called Waugh's Ford, where the rapids provided shallow water with a rocky bottom for crossing by foot and for animals and wagons. A rock on the riverbank, visible from both sides, indicated the water depth. If it could not be seen, it meant the river was too high to be safely forded. The community built up on both sides of the river, a place where local people came to have grain ground at the water mill established there and where wagons traveling between Fredericksburg and the Shenandoah Valley often camped overnight.

The Peyton name first showed up in the area in 1815 when John Peyton took charge of Central Mill, owned then by the Spottswood and Taliaferro families. He and his bride, Lydia Snyder Peyton, lived in the miller's house, constructed around 1772, one of three dwellings

Old caboose at the Rapidan Freight Station.

used by the miller and mill hands, and the oldest building in the area still standing. Lydia, whose family was part of the eighteenth-century German settlement at Hebron in Madison County, bore twelve children, all of whom lived to maturity, and she died at one hundred years and twenty-two days old. She was recorded in a local newspaper a few days before that date as having "remained active with several of her teeth, and her eyesight is quite good, although her hearing is somewhat impaired. She has never eaten more than two meals a day and never wore a corset." John and Lydia's family firmly established the Peyton name in Rapidan and other parts of the world. Ellen estimated that there are about seven hundred descendants of their family.

In 1816, John joined with Revolutionary War general Lawrence T. Dade to start a mill upriver from Waugh's Ford, at Woodberry Forest, three miles from the town of Orange. He was able to buy the mill from Dade, and the site became known as Peyton's Ford.

Floods and debts hounded the business, but a patent was granted to John in 1825 for a fan and screen to clean the milled grains. It was signed by then president John Quincy Adams, Secretary of State Henry Clay and William Wirt of the town of Madison as U.S. attorney. An original copy is on file in the Orange County Historical Society.

The mill at Rapidan continued to flourish under various owners, and it and the churches located there stapled the community together, uniting the local families.

Through the years, these families have become interconnected, evidenced by names in the cemeteries at Waddell Presbyterian and Emmanuel Episcopal Churches. Actually, the Episcopal church is located on the north side of the river, which puts it in Culpeper County. But that is a technicality. County lines are for governments, not for the hearts and minds of the people.

At the organizational meeting establishing Waddell Presbyterian Church in 1877, both Holladays and Peytons held prominent positions. H.T. Holladay was elected elder and served as such for thirty-four years until his death in 1910. George Q. Peyton was elected deacon. He became clerk of sessions in 1880 and filled that position until just before his death in 1932. A

Peyton family tombstones.

talented builder, he constructed several of the remaining homes in the area and also built the pulpit and three chairs still in use in the church. Tombstones of both Peyton and Holladay and their wives are in the cemetery.

The life of the village experienced a distinct change in December 1853 when the Orange and Alexandria Railroad bridged the river to link by rail the towns of Orange and Culpeper. The livery stable and stagecoach stop gave way to growing technology in travel and communication when the railroad company constructed a telegraph office, a passenger station and a freight depot that shipped local wood and wood products.

The community also got a new name when the railroad designated the stop the Rapid Ann Station. There are several conflicting theories as to the spelling of the name, and how and why it changed, but a post office was established there a month later, in January 1854, designated the Rapid Ann Station Post Office. "Station" was eventually dropped from the name in 1886, and the village was officially known as Rapid Ann, eventually spelled as Rapidan.

Favorite Civil War stories—along with other history recorded in Dr. Alan Shotwell's book, *Rapidan Communities*—recall the "International Boundary" established along the banks of the river in the winter of 1963–64. Stories persevere of soldiers, clad in blue uniform on the north side and gray on the south, sometimes singing together and trading food items at night while shooting at one another intermittently during the day. Although skirmishing occurred on both sides of the river, there was no major conflict at the site.

Traumatic events did happen, however. John William Peyton recorded on September 19: "We awoke this morning by smoke of Mr. Holladay's mill, fired by the Yankees. They burnt our house, depot, store houses, bridge and water station. Carried off Capt. Jones, Mr. Nalle, Mr. Boswell and several others."

Farm animals, orchards and fields were raided, and life went on. The wounded were cared for, Confederate officers were entertained at local homes and the children went out to collect chinquapins in the woods.

Ellen recalled seeing the remains of military breastworks on both sides of the river as late as the 1930s before they were destroyed by plows. Floods also turned up artifacts from the war, and in 1978, a live Yankee "Schenkl shell" was found at the Episcopal rectory.

By 1880, a bridge across the river at Rapidan had been built by the railroad, and Dr. Shotwell told the story of Oscar Bresee opting to use it one day instead of fording the river. "[He] was caught as two trains arrived at his position at the same time. He had to hang onto a sand barrel to avoid being crushed. He decided to build a private, arched, single-span bridge a mile downriver from the railroad bridge and a mile upriver from the mill, for his own use." It survived until the flood of 1932 and was not rebuilt.

The river is not kind to bridges. Many of the newly constructed county bridges crossing the river were taken out on April 2, 1886, an event repeated in June 1889. Floods on the Rapidan are legendary, and they are recorded in local memory as twenty-, fifty- and one-hundred-year floods. However, the last and largest inundation, Ellen noted, was "a 500-year flood in 1995."

The bridges were restored and served well, however, and passenger trains brought well-known people to cross the river at Rapidan. When the train stopped to let the engine take on water and coal, a closer look at the village may have been enjoyed by President Cleveland in 1887, the Theodore Roosevelt family in 1902 and President Wilson in 1913.

The Roosevelt family, consisting of the president, Mrs. Roosevelt and four of their children, made up the only presidential party to visit in Rapidan, however, and they spent time as guests of Joseph Wilmer on several occasions.

Perhaps these visits were memories held by Miss Ellen Lovell Peyton, who lived until 1997, when she died at the age of 104.

"Everybody loved Miss Ellen," continued her namesake. "She kept her natural dark brown hair, all of her own teeth, and still had a bright mind at the age of 102. The only time she ever traveled more than four miles from her home was when she went to Charlottesville to vote for a classmate of her husband's who was running for office. She was the former bank manager and postmaster in Rapidan and insisted on the title of 'Postmaster.' She said she never was anyone's mistress."

Miss Ellen's residence, Old Home, was inherited by her niece, Lucy Ann Taylor Grimm. It was built in 1854 for her great-grandfather and burned by the Yankees. It was reconstructed in 1866 by William Snyder Peyton and his sons, including the skilled builder George Q. Peyton, whose work lives on in several of the large homes in the area, including Windy Hill, which he built for himself and his wife, the former Hilda Holladay. Windy Hill also has remained in the Peyton family for three consecutive generations through Elsie Peyton Jarvis, granddaughter of the builder. Several pieces of furniture also built by George Q. Peyton remain in the house.

Ellen estimated that at present there are twenty-four Peytons in five homes in the area. The Peyton name, however, is dwindling from Ellen's line, and for a simple reason. "We kept having girl children. No boys to carry on the name. The grandmothers lived forever, though," she said.

She cited one-hundred-year-old Lydia Snyder Peyton, wife of miller John Peyton, whose family was one of the early seventeenth-century German settlers in Madison County. "She was a widow for forty years. We have a picture of her taken in 1895 when she was two years old, and one of her grand-nieces wearing the same dress and sitting in the same chair."

It is estimated that the population of Rapidan peaked at about 150 people between 1930 and 1950, when the village consisted of three stores, a garage and gas station, a bank, a post office, a school, a railroad depot and a pool hall.

The post office was built for joint occupancy with the State Bank of Rapidan in 1914. It had space for the bank and post office on the first floor and an apartment for the superintendent on the second. The bank was closed in 1945, but the original vault and safe are still there, and the post office continues to do business.

The formerly mentioned "Miss Ellen" Peyton, who had served as the postmaster from 1945 to 1963, was preceded by sixty-eight consecutive years of Peyton family postmasters. They were William S. Peyton, who was there from 1854 to 1864; John W. Peyton, who served until 1915; and George W. Peyton, who worked there until 1922.

Two of the original railroad buildings still remain in the village. One is the passenger station that today is a private residence. The other is the depot. The little schoolhouse at Rapidan is another of the surviving reminders of earlier times in its community.

For more than a century, these structures and others have stayed true to their architectural heritage and remained an integral part of Rapidan's slowly evolving history. Strong community loyalty and values give strong chances that tiny Rapidan will survive.

Rapidan's Schoolhouse

The tiny little one-room schoolhouse in Rapidan has wandered all over the village in five different locations and has served several purposes during its long life, but its architectural and historical integrity remain staunchly intact.

Owned now by the Rapidan Foundation, it was constructed in 1887 by Reverend Mosely Murray, at a cost of $135, as a place to school his eight children. It was built on the lawn of the rectory on Gospel Hill, so named because the rector, along with a retired Presbyterian minister and two deacons, had homes there.

Murray lived on the Orange County side of the Rapidan River but served as rector at Emmanuel Episcopal Church across the river in Culpeper County.

An act to provide free public schooling was passed by Congress in 1868, but people in sparsely populated areas still took on the responsibility to educate their own (and sometimes their neighbors') children.

The first public schooling in Rapidan was held in homes and in the railroad station. At that time, the little schoolhouse, which had ceased being a schoolroom in 1904, was moved down from Gospel Hill to become the village library.

When the first public school building opened in the area in the 1920s, the old schoolhouse was moved by a team of horses across the road to be adjacent to the new school building. There it had various uses as a library and an infirmary, and in the summers it was returned to its original purpose to serve the daily vacation Bible school.

It was relocated about two hundred yards from its present site when a larger public school building was constructed, and it survived even when that building was demolished. For the next forty years, it served as a storage building.

In 1984, the owners of the property on which the schoolhouse was located offered it to the Rapidan Foundation. Members of that organization decided that they had been made an offer they couldn't with any conscience refuse, so the little schoolhouse made its fourth and final move—so far—a few hundred feet to its present location.

Volunteers made the necessary repairs, which were surprisingly few: paint, a new roof, a board here and there and reproductions to replace two of the four arches on the front porch with their whimsical shamrock-shaped cutouts. Miraculously, the wavy amber, green, gold and clear rectangular window panes had survived all the transporting.

There is a small foyer inside the structure's only exterior door that has a closet with a wooden grill above the door, possibly used as a storage closet. Inside the schoolroom are holes in the back wall that held a coat rack. No electrical wiring has ever been installed, and heat came from a little stove on the south side of the room. A water bucket and dipper also were provided.

The wall students faced has diagonal paneling above the chair railing. A reproduction of the American flag used from 1877 to 1890 is displayed there. A small diamond-shaped window with colored panes is also high on that wall, below the exposed roof beams.

The only original furnishing is a long bench under the windows on the north side of the room. Other objects, including some books and a table, desk and bookcase, are of the period, donated by members of the community.

The student desks and the benches long enough to accommodate two or more children were constructed as pieces appropriate to the era by students at Orange County High School in 1997. The student furniture was used that year to present a living history program, with

Rapidan School interior.

local youngsters in period clothing. The students did English and math lessons and used some old maxims and riddles.

"We played outdoor games and there were some mischievous doings, like throwing a [rubber] snake in the schoolhouse window," said Suzanne Shotwell, who portrayed a teacher at the event. "I think it probably was pretty close to an average school day for the time. It was fun bringing that time period to life, and it was a meaningful experience for everyone in it."

A guest book reveals notes, one in Latin, that indicate that visitors also find meaning in the old school. One woman, driving across the country, stopped in at 6:00 a.m. and left a note declaring it "an incredible experience."

Nothing ever has been taken from the building. In fact, sometimes people leave money for its maintenance, says Ellen Donnelly, a Rapidan Foundation member. The foundation draws on a memorial fund for maintenance costs.

Are its journeys finished? Who knows, but for more than one hundred years, the little building has been part of Rapidan's changing history. Chances are that it will survive.

Waddell Memorial Presbyterian Church

The first view of Waddell Memorial Church is always a surprise, somehow. Situated on a hill in the village of Rapidan, its thirty-six slender spires, as pointed as newly sharpened pencils, soar toward the sky, bringing the viewer's spirits along.

Built in 1870, it is listed on the Virginia Historic Landmarks Registry and has been called the state's finest example of Carpenter Gothic architecture. The board-and-batten structure, using local poplar lumber, was built under the supervision of carpenter architect John Gibson from a design by J.B. Danforth of Richmond, whose drawings are held by the church.

About 135 years later, its first major preservation and restoration efforts kept it from destruction by time and termites. Issues to be dealt with included weakened beams, a leaking roof and rotting spires, as well as the removal of three beehives that sent rivulets of honey creeping down the inside walls and inspired one communicant to record in a hymnal a "bee count" of the number of flying insects circulating during a service.

Inside, the pews on either side of the central aisle are lit by arched double-hung windows with clear panes. Air conditioning eliminated the need to raise those windows on warm mornings, "But," said one member, "in the spring and fall, we still open them to let in the country sounds."

In the pulpit is a journalism professor, a stonemason, a blacksmith, an author of several books and a professional restorer of old buildings, all in the person of Pastor Charles MacRaven, who goes by "Mac."

A vigorous and intense man, Pastor MacRaven began his religious training twenty years ago, and he and his wife, Linda, have five children. Their daughter Ashley studied architecture at Virginia Tech, specializing in commercial interiors, and while working for a design firm in Charlottesville, she helped with the restoration of the church. Their other four children also have done mission work.

In addition to his writing and duties at Waddell, the pastor has an architectural restoration business. "I've been restoring all my life," he said, "starting with a log cabin when I was eleven years old." His publications are how-to books on stonework and blacksmithing, as well as one in multiple printings here and abroad on log houses.

His sermons are short, well thought out, applicable to daily life and delivered extemporaneously. He never writes them out. "Notes confuse me," he said.

Nancy and Alan Knewstep are an active part of the congregation. Nancy is one of the members who was raised in the church, "baptized, married and will be buried here." She and Alan have their plot designated in the churchyard. "We realized we might run out of room there, so we reserved our space," said Alan, who is treasurer for the church, is much involved in its restoration and is a dedicated steward of the cemetery.

Alan was strongly instrumental in the $117,000 exterior restoration of the structure, funded by a letter campaign in which Nancy was much involved, writing not only to local people but also to those who had moved away. The presbytery also responded generously with a $5,000 grant.

Phases one and two of the restoration repaired the front steeple and two wings facing the road, put metal caps on the spires, replaced window panes with old glass and relocated the bee colonies. Phase three addressed the fellowship hall, built onto the rear of the original structure in 1958.

The back wall was the first repair job there. "It was built resting on the ground," said Alan, "and the termite damage was so bad it was ready to fall down, right onto the Reverend Waddell's grave!"

Electrical wiring was also updated. Alan told of a roofer who had gone into the attic space and heard some mysterious zapping sounds. To his horror, he found a live extension cord snapping sparks that somehow, for who knows how long, had failed to ignite the structure.

With such history, luck and determination from a dedicated congregation, Waddell Memorial Church surely is destined to be safe at least for another century and a half.

The Blind Preacher

Waddell Presbyterian Church was named to honor Reverend James Waddell, known as the "Blind Preacher."

Born in Ulster, Ireland, Waddell (he preferred it to be spelled "Waddel") moved with his family to Pennsylvania when he was very young. He overcame at least two serious difficulties in his lifetime, the first being an accident when he and his brothers were hunting and tried to cut into a tree to reach a rabbit. James's hand was in the way when his brother brought the axe down and severed his fingers and the lower part of his hand. The hand was bandaged together and reattached, but the severed part never grew in size.

Also, his eyesight became progressively dimmed over the years, caused by cataracts that fully developed in both eyes by the time he was fifty-nine years old. An operation by doctors in Frederick, Maryland, was only partially and temporarily successful, and the cataracts returned. He was totally blind for the rest of his life and became widely known and highly respected as the "Blind Preacher."

Waddell was described by his two sons-in-law, both Presbyterian ministers, as being "tall, slender, erect in general deportment, dignified and commanding, but remarkable for politeness and gentlemanly manner. He had a high face, high forehead, Grecian nose, blue eyes and a small mouth and chin. He was a man of most affectionate disposition and in his treatment of strangers was remarkably courteous. In the expression of his own opinions, he was as free and independent as any man I ever knew."

In his student days, he studied at a seminary in Lancaster County, Pennsylvania, and at the age of nineteen started out for South Carolina to finish his theological studies.

Passing through Virginia on the way, however, he met Reverend Samuel Davies in Louisa County and through him was offered a position as instructor at Reverend John Todd's school at Paynes' Mill near Orchid. He continued his theological studies with Reverend Todd and was ordained by the Hanover Presbytery on April 28, 1761.

He built a strong friendship with Reverend Davies, who later was named president of the University of New Jersey, now Princeton University, and also eventually became close friends with Patrick Henry and James Madison, as well as teacher for James Barbour, Virginia governor and founder of Barboursville.

In 1762, the young Waddell was persuaded by Colonel James Gordon to accept a call at Lancaster and Northumberland Counties, and six years later, he and Gordon's daughter, Mary, were wed. Two of their nine children were born there, with three more after they moved in 1776 to Augusta County, where Waddell was the supply minister at Tinkling Spring Church.

The remaining four children were born when the Waddells returned to the Piedmont area, where they built their home, Hopewell. He preached in and around Charlottesville and built the Belle Grove Church half a mile northeast of the crossroads tavern owned by his brother-in-law, Nathaniel Gordon, for whom the town of Gordonsville was named.

In 1786, the Episcopalians in the town of Orange, then known as Orange Court House, persuaded him to preach for them, since no Episcopal ministers were available. He complied and served for two years.

His congregation at Belle Grove was visited in 1803 by William Wirt, later U.S. attorney general and originator of the myth about George Washington and the cherry tree. Wirt was so overcome by the experience that he later wrote a flowery description, stating in part, "You are to bring before you the venerable figure of the preacher; his blindness constantly recalling to your recollection old Homer, Ossian and Milton…you are to imagine that you hear his slow, solemn, well accented enunciation, his voice of affecting trembling melody; you are to remember the pitch of passion and enthusiasm to which the congregation were raised...I had never seen, in any orator, such a union of simplicity and majesty." Wirt later told Waddell's grandson that he had fallen short in the description of his grandfather.

This is not to say that Waddell was without criticism from his associates. When he was at Tinkling Spring, he caused controversy when he said that one of the elders of his congregation was not setting a good example to young people by riding his horse so fast, especially on a Sunday.

Another time, some church members were scandalized at Waddell's luxury of drinking hot coffee on Sunday mornings. Again, in Louisa, he was accused of "being an advocate of fashionable amusements" by letting his daughters learn to dance the minuet.

Rapidan tombstone.

Waddell Church, Rapidan.

Reverend Waddell died on September 17, 1805, and was buried in the garden at his home, Hopewell. Seventy-six years later, his heirs complied with the request to move his body to Waddell Churchyard, and on March 31, 1881, that was accomplished. One of his grandsons preached the service the day he was interred there.

The Belle Grove church became inactive and was demolished in 1854. A historical marker on Route 15 near Gordonsville designates its site. The lumber was salvaged and sold to a black preacher, and it is believed he used it to build another church.

The Orange Painted
School Bus

G rowing up in Rapidan, Alan Shotwell and his contemporaries rode for forty minutes over roughly paved roads in a bus painted bright orange to go to school in the town of Orange.

"Until the late 1930s or early '40s, the buses were privately owned," he said. "They had three rows of benches, with two aisles running the length of the vehicle that seated four rows of kids. Those sitting along the window row could lean against the side of the bus, but the ones on the middle bench sat in two rows, back to back, facing the windows." The benches were removable so that the vehicle could be used for other purposes during the summer months.

"We boys aided and abetted the driver and tried to get him to go fast over the bumps on the old Willis Ford bridge," Shotwell said. "If you were sitting on the back seat, which you were not supposed to do, you could catapult up to bump your head on the roof to the applause of the whole bus."

The driver was one of the high school students, and he was responsible for keeping the bus clean inside and out, so he washed it regularly and made sure that there wasn't a lot of trash left to pick up. His word was law. "If anyone used bad language, he made them get out and walk." Calvin Davis was one of the drivers during Alan's elementary school days, and later he cut Alan's hair in the barbershop on Main Street in Orange.

Rapidan's orange school bus. *Courtesy of Alan Shotwell.*

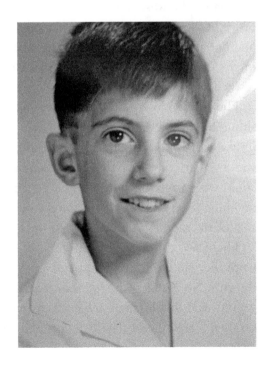

A young Alan Shotwell.
Courtesy of Alan Shotwell.

Calvin had a sense of humor. "Ned Coleman had this little black-and-white dog that used to chase our bus. It was a little rat dog, maybe some sort of Jack Russell cross. Every once in a while, Calvin would let the dog catch up even with the bus, barking and threatening to bite the tires when it slowed down. Then he would cut the engine off for a few seconds and turn it back on, giving the biggest backfire he could get away with," said Shotwell. "That dog would jump in the air yelping, do a few back flips, hit the ground rolling and then check himself for missing parts. Finally, he would get up running and finish chasing us off, always believing he had won because we ran away. His courage made him think he was the biggest dog in Rapidan. Unfortunately, we couldn't get Calvin to do this trick very often. The school board got suspicious after replacing so many bus mufflers."

The driver didn't have to do all the discipline, however. Alan remembers that the older kids took responsibility for the younger ones. If a small child needed help, he got it, and there was no bullying.

The school's Safety Patrol was another guardian feature and a badge of honor—literally. The designated students, of whom Alan was one, had a badge to pin on and a white belt with a cross strap over one shoulder that had to be washed every week. He was one of those responsible for order in the schoolyard, having the children line up for the correct bus and finding anyone who was missing. His authority, however, evaporated on the bus. "Everyone knew me, and the older kids would ignore me and just tell me to sit down."

The bus windows would push up to open, and in warm weather, those sitting by the window could put an arm out and scoop in some cool air until the driver noticed. They might also be able to sneak a wave out the window to friends, like Miss Lizzie Armentrout, who, after her retirement, could wave from her house to the passing bus. "She had seventh grade and taught generations of my family. I'd hear my behavior compared to that of my mother, Alice Taylor, or my Uncle Garland."

There was an undesignated and self-regulated dress code. Everyone wore nice clothes, shirts and pants for the boys and dresses, always, for the girls. No T-shirts with logos or messages on them and no shorts.

Alan said that his goal in life was to avoid boredom. "It was harder to do then." His typical day included feeding the dog, the horses, the two milk cows, the ducks, the domino and bantam chickens and the big red rooster, along with chopping wood after school in the winter. His trips on the orange painted bus were escapes from the sameness of chores and a highlight of the beginning and end of the school day, making warmly kept memories of his years growing up.

Alan Shotwell, doctor of optometry, has written a book, The History of Rapidan, *which is available at the James Madison Museum.*

The Ruins

Home of James Barbour

The empty shell of the home built for James Barbour between 1814 and 1822 awes as many visitors today as it did before it was burned out, with its undisputed claim to have indeed been personally designed by Thomas Jefferson.

In earlier times, guests riding or driving their horses up to the imposing brick structure were greeted by the first glimpse of the soaring chimneys that still beckon over the treetops. The large field on the front, or north, side of the house was the site of an oval quarter-mile track meant to provide for and indulge the traditional Virginia passion for horse racing.

An opening through ancient boxwood shrubs presents a breathtaking view of the architecturally stabilized outer walls of the structure. The vacant windows look into empty space, leaving the viewer with a lingering sense of poignancy. Marks on the bricks of the interior walls show where beams were fitted and where lintel pediments and fireplace surrounds were located. The site has been designated as a Virginia historic landmark.

Barbour called his estate Barboursville. Today, the remains of the once elegant mansion are known locally and familiarly as "The Ruins," and the surroundings now serve as a site for gatherings and weddings.

To the east, hundreds of strictly disciplined but lovingly cared-for grapevines march rhythmically across adjacent slopes. The grapes will be

The Ruins, Barboursville.

turned into award-winning wines by the present owner of the property, Barboursville Vineyards.

Jefferson drew plans for Barboursville in 1817—and also, it is thought, for two other structures in which the family lived while the house was being built. They are located on the west side of the main house and later were joined and used to house the servants. The structure now is the residence for the present property owners, with three B&B suites available to the public.

The manor house is thought of as one of Jefferson's most successful creations and was called one of the most beautiful homes in the Virginia Piedmont area. The warm red bricks were made from local clay, with large pedimented porticos and massive white Doric columns.

The large north portico was the main entrance into the hexagonal salon, whose shape still is visible. It soared upward to the mansard roof, with an elegant domed ceiling. Jefferson had planned the dome to extend above the roof, as at Monticello, but apparently Barbour felt differently since it never was built that way.

Two corridors with narrow stairways, another Monticello touch, extended transversely from either side through the house in the rectangular room behind the octagonal salon. Doorways on both the north and south sides also passed centrally through the structure, giving easy access to all of the downstairs rooms. The drawing room and study had fireplaces, but heating in the upstairs bedrooms exhibited the cutting edge of technology: wood-burning Benjamin Franklin stoves.

The mansion was the most elaborate dwelling in the area and, along with the outbuildings, was assessed in local tax records at $20,000, more than twice that of Montpelier, the next-highest appraisal in the county.

Off the south portico was a three-acre rectangular garden with a brick serpentine wall. Walks were lined with grass, and double rows of boxwood shrubs crisscrossed the garden. An especially arresting feature was a meandering flower-bordered stream that had three rustic bridges. To the east were the icehouse, carriage house, barns and a long row of handsome stables.

After Barbour's death, his son, James Barbour Jr., inherited and continued to live in the house for forty-two years until it caught fire from lighted candles on the Christmas tree and was destroyed on December 25, 1884.

James Barbour was one of Orange County's most noteworthy citizens. His Scottish grandfather, also named James, was a prosperous merchant who settled in King and Queen County in the late seventeenth century. His son, Thomas, was heir to a sizeable inheritance that unfortunately was squandered before he reached his majority and could claim it. He was able to acquire property on the Rapidan River in what then was Spotsylvania County and was the first permanent settler of what was to become Orange County, preceding the Madisons by three years.

Following the traditional Virginia path of upward mobility, he served on the vestry at St. Mark's Parish, served as Orange County sheriff, became a court justice and was elected to the Virginia House of Burgesses in the Williamsburg capitol, where he served from 1760 to 1775, the crucial years that led to the American Revolution.

James, his eldest surviving son, was born in 1775, followed by three sisters and a brother, Philip Pendleton Barbour, who later became a U.S. senator and associate justice of the supreme court.

Financial reversals after the Revolution precluded James's education away from home, as expected from most of his social class. Instead, he was tutored at home by the highly respected Presbyterian minister James Waddell, for whom a church is named in Rapidan. Waddell's legendary skills in oratory apparently inspired James's passion in that art, and it served him well in his career.

Rather than attend law school, he followed early traditions of becoming a lawyer by "reading the law," the equivalent of serving an apprenticeship, with an established member of the bar in Richmond in 1791. He returned home after passing his bar exam and began his legal practice.

Described by a contemporary as being nearly six feet tall, with a large head and shoulders, he was a handsome man, athletic, erect and muscular. He began purchasing property in southern Orange County in 1800, and by the time he started to build his house, he owned forty thousand acres. This was in addition to five thousand acres in Kentucky given to him by his father when he married his cousin, Lucy Johnson.

In the meantime, he had become active in politics, serving as deputy sheriff in Orange County and being elected to the Virginia Assembly in April 1798. In January 1811, during the presidency of neighbor James Madison, he was appointed by his fellow legislators to fulfill the unexpired term of the elected governor, George William Smith, who had died in office.

He and Lucy were the first to live in the newly built governor's mansion in Richmond, and a few pieces of their furniture are still there. Legend has it that the couple began a custom of always having bowls of punch in the reception rooms, ready for guests who might drop in, and that often included the legislators.

Barbour made significant changes in Virginia government, including the radical liberal movement of sponsoring the state's anti-dueling law, said to be one the of the most stringent and effective legislative acts ever passed at the time. He considered as his greatest accomplishment, however, the creation of a board of school commissioners in each county and the forming of the General Library Fund of Virginia for the education of poor children.

He was elected by the Virginia legislators to the U.S. Senate in 1815. He held that post for ten years, during which time his concerns included the "Missouri Question" and the abolition of imprisonment for debt. He was chairman of the Committee of Foreign Affairs and often served as president pro tem of the Senate.

President John Quincy Adams appointed Barbour as secretary of war, and then he served as minister to Great Britain. He and Lucy took their children—James, Cornelia and Benjamin Johnson—with them, and Barbour also traveled to LaGrange in France, where he visited the Marquis de Lafayette, whom he had met when the general had returned to Orange County for a visit after the Revolutionary War. The Barbours brought furniture back from France for their Virginia home, some pieces of which are still owned by descendants.

While in Europe, he found much mutual love of fine horses among the British, and when he came home, he brought Truffles, a stallion of the finest English stock, and five thoroughbred mares to Barboursville to found his own extraordinary stables that eventually numbered up to fifty. The horses added to the breeding stock on this side of the Atlantic and became an important source of income. Truffles, for instance, earned $4,678 in stud fees in 1800, his first year at Barboursville plantation.

Barbour retired when he came back from England as one of the wealthiest planters in Piedmont Virginia. By 1830, he owned thousands of acres of property in this and other southern states.

He died from an unspecified illness on June 7, 1842, three days before his sixty-eighth birthday. He is buried at Barboursville, a brass plaque is placed on a brick wall behind his grave. It lists his accomplishments, although his own request was simpler: "If anything is put over me, let it be of the plainest granite, with no other claim than this: 'Here lies James Barbour, originator of the Library Fund of Virginia.'"

The Village of Barboursville

James Barbour deeded several acres of his Barboursville estate where two major roads (Routes 20 and 33) meet with the purpose of establishing a village with the same name, hoping that it would draw and support a post office and a train station. Those two conveniences did, in fact, become realities, and the area eventually encompassed seven hotels and boardinghouses, two livery stables and three stores. About half a mile down Route 33 is the site where a public high school and elementary school were constructed by the WPA in the 1930s. The elementary school that held grades one through three, the cafeteria and the auditorium was turned, in 1972, into the longest-running community theater in the Piedmont area, Four County Players, which produces four to five shows per season. The high school building has been torn down, but the athletic field is still in use for local field sports.

When rail service ended, the town rapidly declined until the 1970s, by which time all that remained were former boardinghouses converted to private residences or apartments, as well as three businesses: Sheepman Supply, Mundy's Auto Repair and Elsie's Antiques.

In 1976, artist Fred Nichols and his wife, Beth, purchased the old Williams General Store. They turned it into their home, studio and art gallery, where Fred began producing paintings and silkscreen prints of scenes in the Blue Ridge Mountains, for which he has achieved international recognition. Beth, acting as art marketer and exhibit designer, produces shows that include Fred's work, as well as that of other local artists. They expanded their gallery space into the old Estes-Sparks Hotel in 1998.

During this time, the Zonin family, owners of the largest wine company in Italy, had purchased land formerly belonging to the Barbours and established the first vineyards in the area. By the mid-1900s, there was a total of three local vineyards, all with notable products.

About the Author

Patricia LaLand, a native of Seattle, graduated from the University of Washington with a BA in speech therapy. After marriage to an army officer, five moves and two children, they found themselves stationed in Virginia, where she began working as a tour guide at Colonial Williamsburg. She edited the employees' newspaper and then moved to the press bureau as a writer.

She became the administrator of the President's House at the College of William and Mary and took that same position at Mount Clare Mansion in Baltimore.

Returning to Virginia, she became the assistant director of James Madison's Montpelier in Orange for the National Trust for Historic Preservation and continued free-lance writing for major consumer magazines, for which she was recognized with awards from Virginia Press Women and the National Federation of Press Women.

For several years, she wrote a history column for *O.C. Magazine* and for the *Fredericksburg Free Lance-Star* that led to this book. She has delighted in travel and has visited every continent except Antarctica.

"Life," she says, "leads to unexpected tests and pleasures."

Visit us at
www.historypress.net

CPSIA information can be obtained
at www.ICGtesting.com
Printed in the USA
BVHW041203311218
536774BV00019BB/1510/P